# Looking
# Closer:
Kevin Spacey, the first 50 years

# Also by Robin Tamblyn

*King of Hollywood* (2003)

*Velocity* (2004)

*coupling* (2005)

*Medium Everything: collected writings* (2006)

*Dark Muse: Kevin Spacey, Fan Faction,
and the Weinstein Effect* (2019)

# Looking
# Closer:

## Kevin Spacey, the first 50 years

ROBIN TAMBLYN

iUniverse®

# LOOKING CLOSER: KEVIN SPACEY, THE FIRST 50 YEARS

iUniverse books may be ordered through booksellers or by contacting:

iUniverse
1663 Liberty Drive
Bloomington, IN 47403
www.iuniverse.com
844-349-9409

Because of the dynamic nature of the Internet, any web addresses or links contained in this book may have changed since publication and may no longer be valid. The views expressed in this work are solely those of the author and do not necessarily reflect the views of the publisher, and the publisher hereby disclaims any responsibility for them.

Any people depicted in stock imagery provided by Getty Images are models, and such images are being used for illustrative purposes only. Certain stock imagery © Getty Images.

ISBN: 978-1-6632-3271-7 (sc)
ISBN: 978-1-6632-3270-0 (e)

Print information available on the last page.

iUniverse rev. date: 11/29/2021

# Contents

*For Mini*
*—long may her adventures continue!*

spacy *adj.* **1.** in a daze, out of touch with reality, eccentric.
**2.** exhibiting characteristics actually or figuratively reminiscent of those experienced when taking a hallucinogen.
*See also* SPACEY.[1]


MILO
What exactly is a games-playing person?

ANDREW
He's the complete man—a man of reason and imagination; of potent passions and bright fancies. He's joyous and unrepenting. His weapons are the openness of a child and the cunning of a pike and with them he faces out the black terrors of life. For me personally he is a man who dares to live his life without the crutch of domestic tension. You see, at bottom, I'm rather a solitary man. An arrangement of clouds, the secret mystery of landscape, a game of intrigue and revelation, mean more to me than people—even the ones I'm supposed to be in love with. I've never met a woman to whom the claims of intellect were as absolute as they are to me. For a long time I was reticent about all this, knowing that most people would mistake my adroit heart for one of polished stone. But it doesn't worry me any longer. I'm out in the open. I've turned my whole life into one great work of happy invention.

MILO
And you think I'm like this?

ANDREW
Yes, I do.

MILO
You're wrong.[2]

# Author's Note

*"A book about me? It seems sort of odd…"*
–Kevin Spacey's response to the question "Ever consider
writing an autobiography?" (2003)[3]

I first started work on *Looking Closer* in early July 2009 and had completed the final published draft by late November. The short period of time between these two dates should give an indication of the purpose of the book: although I have discussed several of his major projects on celluloid and stage, it does not provide a complete list or conclusive appraisal of every film, play or television production involving Spacey, nor does it constitute the definitive record of his life–my aim was to take a peek behind the Spacey "mask" rather than rip it off entirely.

The majority of material was taken from secondary sources, duly acknowledged, and with the exception of Kevin's brother Randy, who provided some background data with regard to Kevin's ancestry and childhood through access to his as-yet-unreleased biography, no direct contact with Spacey's family or associates was made for the book. While I have kept to standard British English for the main text, where direct quotations from foreign sources have been used I have retained the original American English spelling. Any profanity deletions have also been reproduced unaltered.

Robin Tamblyn
December 2009

*Looking Closer* has been revised several times since its initial publication in 2010, both to resolve small inaccuracies within the text and to add further information about Spacey from additional interviews and other contemporary sources that were not previously available to me. This latest edition includes information about Kevin's family background taken from the Ancestry website and I have also removed a reference incorrectly describing the actor John Graham Spacey as Kevin's "great-great-uncle."

On 29 October 2017, Kevin Spacey's world changed forever when *Star Trek: Discovery* star Anthony Rapp claimed that the older actor had made an unwelcome sexual advance towards him during a cast party at Spacey's apartment in 1986, when Kevin was 26 and Rapp just fourteen. In a now-infamous Twitter post, Spacey claimed not to remember the incident but apologised to Rapp for any wrongdoing. He also took the opportunity to confirm his sexual orientation for the first time, stating that: "As those closest to me know, in my life I have had relationships with both men and women. I have loved and had romantic encounters with men throughout my life, and I choose now to live as a gay man."[4]

In this latest edition, I have chosen to retain the original 2010 copyright, so there are no references to Spacey's private or professional life post-2009. Further information regarding the recent allegations of sexual harassment and assault made against Spacey by multiple men is available in my book *Dark Muse: Kevin Spacey, Fan Faction, and the Weinstein Effect*, which also discusses how his life inspired my previous works of fiction, particularly my 2003 novel *King of Hollywood* and two of the entries in my short story collection *coupling* from 2005.

Robin Tamblyn
October 2021

# Preface
# Inner Spacey

*"I am as much myself on any given day as I can possibly be. I have good days. I have bad days. I have people who piss me off. I have people who make me happy. I am not an image. I am a human being, with as many flaws, foibles, good sides, bad sides, as any other human being, and this idea that somehow I'm a person who shouldn't be perceived as a human being because I'm an actor..."*
—Kevin Spacey (2002)[5]

*"We know more about the surface of Mars than about Spacey's private life."*
—anonymous[6]

By most accounts, Kevin Spacey Fowler was born in New Jersey on 26th July 1959, the third and youngest child of Thomas and Kathleen Fowler. "Spacey," which he would take as his professional surname some twenty years later, was the maiden name of his mother.

So far, so simple.

But…look closer…

Kevin Spacey Fowler? No such person, apparently. His first two names at birth are listed by several sources as "Kevin Matthew."[7] "Fowler" is also a matter of dispute as his father, born Thomas Corden Fowler but known for most of his adult life as Geoff, legally adopted his stepfather's surname of Longshore shortly before joining the army in 1943.[8] And "Spacy" (without the "e") was not Kathleen's family moniker but the maiden name of Geoff's mother, Norma.

Such discrepancies are a part of the life of the man the world now knows as Kevin Spacey. In his dual role as Oscar-winning movie actor and artistic director of London's Old Vic, his name and image are everywhere, yet he remains elusive, enthusiastically promoting his latest film or theatre project while keeping all "personal" enquiries firmly off limits.

So, who is he?

A loner, or a social butterfly?

A theatre luvvie, or Mr. Cinema?

A diva, or down-to-earth?

A playboy, or a family guy?

Media savvy, or naïve to the ways of the Press?

Actually, he is all of these things–and none of them. Over the course of the next ten chapters, this book will explore the career and background of Hollywood's most enigmatic star–a man who so subsumes himself in the roles he plays that outside of them he almost appears not to exist. As *L.A. Confidential* author James Ellroy once observed: "There is something amorphous about the guy...there's a mask that's up when you meet him personally, and I imagine that this helps him when he immerses himself in a character."[9]

"Do not be fooled," warns David Thomson in his Spacey profile in *The New Biographical Dictionary of Film*, "Kevin Fowler is and always was a chronic pretender, a naughty boy, a wicked mimic, and a scathing mind. Keyser Söze indeed! He can be our best actor, but only if we accept that acting is a bag of tricks that leaves scant room for becoming a real and considerate human being."[10]

When once asked whether he "saw the contract between personal revelation and success," Spacey succinctly replied: "I see it, but I never signed it." He added: "It's not that I want to create some bullshit mystique by maintaining a silence about my personal life, it is just that the less you know about me, the easier it is to convince you that I am that character on screen."[11] But there are so many "Kevin Spaceys" that the opposite is probably true–the more that is revealed about this "human Escher print,"[12] the more multi-facetted and unfathomable he seems.

Interviewing Kevin is a challenge. Many a reporter has come away from a first encounter confident that they have just met the "real" Kevin Spacey, only to be confronted by a completely different persona the next time they see him.[13] "You could spend a lifetime trying to work out Spacey and still be left with loose ends,"[14] as one writer from *The Times* put it in 2002. No one is ever quite what they seem on a Kevin Spacey project, and that includes the man himself.

# Chapter One

# Spacey Origins

*"Your soul comes from the tragedy of your childhood."*
–Don Auippo to Mel Profitt, *Wiseguy* (1988)

*"It's like you know he has this very complicated past, but you don't know what it is…"*
–*The Usual Suspects* director Bryan Singer on Spacey (1997)[15]

While Kevin Spacey is the first bona fide film star to bear the name, he was not the first "Spacey" to appear on the screen. That honour belongs to a distant cousin, John Graham Spacey, born in Tostock, Suffolk, England, in 1897. John, who was raised in Derbyshire and emigrated to the United States in 1920, played small, frequently uncredited roles in over thirty British and American films between 1935 and 1940, notably *Women of Glamour* and *Special Inspector*, before his premature death from a heart attack at the age of 42.[16] He also appeared in John Van Druten's play *There's Always Juliet* at the Ethel Barrymore Theatre on Broadway in 1932: over fifty years later, Kevin would perform in *Hurlyburly* at the same venue.

The branch of the Spacy/Spacey family tree that would eventually produce Kevin first reached American shores in 1768 in the form of nineteen-year-old John S. Spacy from Yorkshire, England, who was deported to the Southern Colonies for sheep-stealing and later served as a private in the 5th Virginia Regiment during the American War of Independence. John's great-great granddaughter, Norma Louise Spacy, was born in 1902 in Memphis, Tennessee. She later moved to Denver, Colorado, where she married Bayard Cecil Fowler in 1923, and on 4th June 1924 gave birth to a son, Thomas Corden.

Norma and Bayard Cecil divorced in December 1926, when little Thomas was two-and-a-half: Fowler senior disappeared from the family archives early on and is not believed to have kept in any contact with his son.[17] Known as "Tom" or "Tommy" as a child, the younger Fowler discarded his middle name of Corden, apparently a tribute to Bayard Cecil's father Cordon Fowler, soon after he reached adulthood and was thereafter known as Thomas Geoffrey, or "Geoff."

Following her divorce, Norma moved to Casper, Wyoming, where she married engineer Willard Breck Longshore, the scion of a once-wealthy dynasty of sheep ranchers that had lost most of their fortune during the 1929 stock market crash. She appears to have been quite the society belle: an account of the Fowler-Longshore wedding in the March 1930 edition of the *Casper Star Tribune* described her as "one of the loveliest young women in Casper" and noted that "the wedding proved most interesting because it joined together one of Casper's most attractive girls to a son of a pioneer family of Casper and Natrona county."[18] No mention is made of Norma's first marriage: her son is merely listed as a wedding guest.

The newlyweds set up home in Los Angeles and had three children together, daughter Nancy in 1932 and twins Stephen and Susan in 1936. Mr. Longshore proved to be a stern parent, especially in regard to his stepson, who found himself increasingly isolated from the family unit once his half-siblings arrived. Geoff later claimed that as a child he had endured frequent beatings from Willard, who would mete out punishment whilst wielding a large board. During high school, Geoff ran two paper routes to help supplement the family income, and was over-burdened by homework, often studying until midnight for the advanced college preparatory classes he took from seventh through twelfth grades.

With no money (he turned all his paper route pay over to his mother), little time for socialising, and an unhappy home life, the teenager–gangly, underweight and badly afflicted by eczema, a skin condition both his sons would later inherit–developed into a lonely, awkward, and somewhat naïve young man. He had few outside interests, though he was a an active member of the Boy Scouts, attaining the rank of Eagle Scout in 1942, and became the drum major of the North Hollywood High School Marching Band the same year.

After graduating from North Hollywood High in April 1943, Geoff, like many thousands of other young American men during the country's participation in World War II, enlisted in the Army. On the way to the induction centre, Norma, well aware that if her firstborn was killed in action it would be easier to obtain death benefits if their surnames matched, insisted he take a detour to a Los Angeles courthouse to legally amend his last name from "Fowler" to "Longshore."

After completing his basic training, Geoff was shipped overseas in 1944 to join the Medical Corps and received an estimated $175-a-month pay, plus savings bonds–a small fortune to the perpetually poverty-stricken youth. His mother demanded he send the money to her to be put into a bank account until he returned home. Ever the dutiful son where Norma was concerned, Geoff complied. He spent some time in Scotland, obtaining a pocket watch that he subsequently wound and wore every day,[19] and England, where he was impressed with what he regarded as its "aristocratic" way of life.[20] He retained an interest in the United Kingdom, later taking his family on annual trips to the U.S. Scottish Games in Los Angeles, where he would dress up in full Highland regalia.

Geoff was stationed in Berlin at the end of the war, assisting with the reparations of the stricken city. Putting his high school French and German classes to somewhat dubious use, he purportedly ran a black market operation (trading in food, clothing, cigarettes and other items on demand) to earn extra cash. Working closely with Berlin's devastated inhabitants had a profound impact on him–sympathy later turned to empathy as he grew to be an ardent admirer of German culture, history and ideology.

"I never saw a concentration camp the whole time I was in Germany," Geoff would later tell his family. "The German people wouldn't have allowed that sort of thing. They're too civilized. This whole Holocaust business is just part of a worldwide Jewish conspiracy. Six million people killed in these so-called death camps! What nonsense! Can you imagine the logistics of trying to get rid of six million bodies?"[21]

His youthful scrawniness gone, Geoff arrived back in the U.S. in April 1946 with one notable souvenir–a Luger pistol–concealed in his duffel bag, and headed straight for the Longshore home in Casper, where Norma and Willard had relocated their family to in the early 1940s, to collect his

Army payments. The expected $5000-plus from his three years of service, however, was nowhere to be seen and his bank account contained only $500. His mother insisted that was all that had ever been received–Geoff suspected otherwise, but let the matter drop.

Unsure of a career path now that he was out of the Army, the young man began attending a local college to improve his prospects. He passed a preliminary entry exam for West Point, but was reportedly denied admission after a distant relative of Willard's intervened to block the application. This incident only fuelled Geoff's burgeoning prejudices, as he thereafter maintained that "some rich Jew with influence"[22] had deprived him of his rightful place at the famous military academy.

With his savings depleted, Geoff soon ran into financial troubles and was forced to ask his stepfather for help. Willard, keen for his stepson to follow him into the oil business, was only prepared to support Geoff if he majored in geology. Having no interest in the subject, Geoff declined the offer and dropped out of school. In late 1947, he moved back to Los Angeles alone and enrolled on a business administration course at Westbury College, a division of the University of Southern California, renting a room in a Westlake Park boarding house from one Harriet Knutson, mother of a sixteen-year-old daughter, Kathleen.

Kathleen Ann Knutson was born on 5th December 1931 in Minneapolis, Minnesota. Like Geoff, she had an unsettled childhood, later recalling that it "was not only disruptive as far as moving...and not having anywhere I could call home, but was also slightly terrifying."[23] As an "army brat" her family was often uprooted and she was raised in a succession of new and unfamiliar places–by graduation she had attended 23 different schools.

Kathleen's mother, Harriet Elizabeth Powell, was born in 1896 in Indiana and had a brief early marriage to a man named Floyd Lovell. Their daughter Elizabeth Jane (1919-94) was a minor musical star in the 1940s, initially billed as "Lovely Jane Lovell" and then as Jane LaVell. Jane performed as a vocalist with orchestral accompaniment at several venues across the Midwestern and Southern United States, such as the Starlight Gardens in Cincinnati and the Van Cleve Hotel in Dayton, Ohio.

In May 1929, Harriet married Allen August Knutson, a charismatic itinerant military mechanic whose parents Olof and Vehelmena had both emigrated from Sweden to Goodhue, Minnesota, in the 1880s. "Knutsen" and "Knudsen" are variant spellings used by the clan, who abandoned the Scandinavian patronymic naming system on arrival in the United States (had this been retained, Allen would have been "Allen Olofsson" and Kathleen "Kathleen Allensdotter"). Harriet gave birth to Kathleen two years later, and the couple subsequently divorced and re-wed each other twice more before finally splitting for good in 1948.

The Knutson household was certainly a volatile one. Harriet's ex-husband, Floyd, would frequently turn up unannounced to pick a quarrel with his former wife. Her twice-widowed, once-divorced mother, Louisa "Lulu" Cole, also lived with the family for several years and had regular sparring matches with Allen, whose frequent periods of drunkenness would result in violent squabbles with Harriet and ejection from the family home.

Sober, Allen would beg Harriet's forgiveness, and a temporary peace would descend until he picked up the bottle again. Young Kathleen–who bore a scar on her knee from a knife hurled by Allen in an alcohol-fuelled rage–kept out of the way of her warring elders as much as possible, spending hours by herself composing poems, reading romance and adventure books or practising the piano. Simultaneously, the young girl began to develop what would later become a highly-refined protective technique: avoidance. If she didn't have to see it, didn't have to hear it, then something disagreeable couldn't affect her.

The Knutsons–minus Lulu–moved to Southern California in the early 1940s. As they were initially unable to find a suitable family house in downtown Los Angeles, Kathleen was sent to stay with Harriet's friend Myrtle Taylor in La Puente, where she was put to work doing all the household chores, forced to wait on Myrtle's lazy teenage daughter whilst trying to dodge her lecherous husband, Marcus. After seven months Kathleen returned home to find that the transfer to L.A. had changed nothing: her father was still drinking, her parents still rowing. She retreated to the vacant lot next door, sitting in the balmy Californian sunshine with her romance novels, hoping and waiting for her own knight in shining armour to come along.

And come along he did. To the sixteen-year-old Kathleen, the taciturn, brooding twenty-three-year-old war veteran lodging upstairs, a clean-living non-smoker who never touched alcohol and was struggling to fund himself through college to pursue his new dream of becoming a writer, was an All-American hero, a different breed of man altogether from her wild, drunken father or the lusty "Uncle" Marcus. Sympathetic to Geoff's financial woes–he helped Harriet with the housework in exchange for a reduction to his rent–Kathleen used her own small allowance to buy him $0.79 hot dinners at the local Thrifty Drug Store when his monthly $75 G.I. Bill payments ran out.

Courtship duly followed, the young couple becoming Mr. and Mrs. Fowler Longshore on 14th February 1949. As Kathleen noted, Harriet was less than pleased with her daughter's decision to wed their erstwhile tenant:

> "I went to Dad to get his consent for marriage…just in case Mother said "no." We got it in writing and had it notarized–my big mistake was in not telling Dad not to tell Mother. He did and it just happened to be the day before Valentine's. Mother put my clothing, books, etc. in a large pile on the front porch and told me to leave. I convinced her to let me stay the night and the next day [Geoff] and I went to have blood tests, took them to the lab to have them checked, got the marriage license and got married just before the Courthouse closed at 4.00 PM. Of course, we had nowhere to live! So much for the "isn't that romantic, you were married on Valentine's Day" comments."[24]

Later that year, Geoff graduated from college and Kathleen graduated from high school. Diplomas in hand, they left their shared fractured, troubled childhoods behind and set out in search of employment. The newlyweds soon settled into the routine of married life, establishing a pattern that remained consistent throughout their forty-plus years together. Whilst Kathleen, who had trained as an executive secretary and even developed her own private shorthand style, seldom had any problem finding positions, Geoff, officially a freelance technical writer, was often out of work for long periods (an early offer of a prestigious job in journalism was lost when his mother refused to loan him $100 to buy a car).

"If you built the F-16," son Kevin later observed, "[Geoff] would have written the manual to tell you how to do that. So it was very boring, technical gobbledegook that he hated doing."[25] Never one for socialising, Geoff retreated to his study, where he would sit behind the locked door for hours with a far-from-innocuous collection of reading materials: Anti-Semitic literature and nudist magazines.[26]

Geoff and Kathleen's eldest child, daughter Julie Ann, was born in Los Angeles on 19th March 1951. The three of them moved to Montrose, Colorado, in 1955, where son Randall Breck (known as Randy) arrived on 23rd January of the following year. Kathleen was still the main breadwinner while Geoff was employed only sporadically, briefly landing a job copywriting for the local newspaper. Like the heroines of her romance novels, though, she nevertheless deferred to her husband in all matters concerning their growing brood.

Soon after Randy's birth, the foursome moved to Brooklyn, New York, then onto South Orange, New Jersey, in early 1959, where Kevin Spacey (or possibly Matthew) Fowler/Longshore was born on 26th July. Photographs of the young Kevin show the chubby toddler already displaying the intense, baleful gaze that would one day become his calling card.

In 1961, the family moved back to the West Coast, initially settling in Santa Monica, California. During the next decade, they would change residences frequently, switching between houses and apartments in Malibu, Thousand Oaks, Wildwood and Canoga Park, with Kathleen's—and much less often Geoff's—monthly pay cheque determining the size and location of their current abode.

Spacey has often spoken of the impact the constant movement had on himself, usually expressing admiration for his mother for "working her ass off"[27] to support her children and deep anger towards his father for forcing him to leave yet another school and set of friends behind:

> "By the time I was 14, I had changed school about 10 times. I was always the new kid on the block. It was great training for me as an actor, but it was terrifying, it was lonely, it was scary. To always

have to make new friends…because my dad was unemployed, we lost the lease on places and we had to move. So there was this upheaval all the time…There were times I was *so* angry with my father for moving us around. I couldn't have done better in his shoes, I suppose…But I remember being very angry nonetheless, and *fucking* pissed off that we were going to move the next day and I was never going to see my new best friend again."[28]

"I was constantly being thrown into a new school, thrown into a new church and the new kid on the block. Always, always, always. Starting over again. I'll never forget this. I remember lying in the bottom of an empty pool with my best friend at the time. I was lying on my back and my friend was lying on his back and we were looking up at the sky, the night before the moving vans were coming. And I remember I was so upset that I was moving. And I must have been nine years old. And I remember crying, lying on my back and there were tears streaming down my face. I remember for several days, I hated my father so much. I hated him for making us move. I hated him for making me go through this fucking ritual of having to start all over again and be the new kid and find a way in and get beaten up."[29]

Kevin's own sense of dislocation may explain why, after the chance reading of an article in a Toronto paper, he felt so "drawn" to the story of tragic Polar-born Minik Wallace. Young Minik was the only survivor of a group of six Inuit who were brought to New York in 1897 by explorer Robert Peary as "live specimens" of Eskimo culture. His return to Greenland in 1909 was far from successful as he had been too long removed from his birthplace to fully re-integrate into the community and he eventually came back to the United States, dying of pneumonia in New Hampshire in 1918.

"Minik had no home," wrote Spacey in his introduction to the 2001 edition of Kenn Harper's biography, "plucked from his own world, never wholly welcomed by another, he was condemned to look forever for what he had lost."[30] Kevin illustrated the parallels with his own situation particularly poignantly a year later: "When some people think of home they think of a place, where they grew up and had all their Thanksgiving dinners and all their Christmas dinners and all their family gatherings and I don't have that."[31]

As young Kathleen Knutson had found, continual house moves make it difficult to maintain friendships. The Fowler siblings had an advantage over their mom (and Minik Wallace) though: they had each other. The three youngsters formed a tight-knit little group, playing games together, going on joint excursions to beaches, parks, museums and zoos, sneaking into their parents' bedroom at Christmas time for a preview of their presents. In a 1984 typewritten letter that she sent to each of her three offspring, Kathleen recalled a seemingly-humorous incident from one Halloween night in Malibu that could have come straight out of a Norman Rockwell storybook:

> "You had all gone out Trick or Treating [and] came home with fairly large bags of "goodies" and we decided to let you do whatever you wanted, just to see the result. Well, every 10 to 15 minutes one of you would ask if it was time to go to bed and we said whenever you felt like it. Then you wanted to know if you had eaten enough of your candy and we told you to eat as much as you wanted. Believe me, you really didn't know what to do; you wanted us to tell you to stop making yourselves sick and go to sleep."[32]

Outwardly, Geoff, Kathleen, Julie, Randy and Kevin were an "ordinary" family, not wealthy but above the poverty line, more settled and secure as a unit than the fractious, forever-at-war Knutson and Longshore clans. Not exactly living the American Dream, perhaps, but on the fringes of it.

Appearances, of course, can be deceptive. By the mid-1960s Geoff Fowler was far from being the dashing squaddie who had first captivated a teenage Kathleen. As older adults, the couple had few shared interests and rarely displayed any outward affection towards one another, not even conversing much except when necessary.

The ever-compliant Kathleen, a good communicator who mixed well in public despite her own early traumas, continued to find gainful employment; her dilettante, reclusive husband continued to cocoon himself in his office with his racist pamphlets and pornographic books, feverishly working on a novel that never materialised. "[He'd] shut the door and be gone for days. My mum would put food down for him, he'd pick it up, take it in and continue writing," Kevin has said. "You weren't allowed in Dad's study. It was his study, his space."[33]

In an interview with *The Mail on Sunday* in April 2004, elder son Randy revealed their dark family secret. As an adolescent, his father had sexually abused him.[34] Like stepfather Willard, Geoff—who once related that he had been molested himself by his Scoutmaster in the late 1930s, dismissing the incident as "no big deal,"[35] was never one to "spare the rod"–"a strict disciplinarian,"[36] as Spacey recalled.

All three children would receive firm chastisement when they misbehaved, though Kevin, as his mother noted in her 1984 letter, "got very few spankings, probably because he "profited by Randall's mistakes" or was just clever enough for us not to find out everything."[37] Randy–who referred to his scabby-skinned father as "The Creature"–bore the brunt of Geoff's brutal desires, enduring a horrific cycle of physical and sexual molestation and rape on regular occasions throughout his childhood and early teenage years.

The youngest member of the family was apparently unaware of his sibling's ordeal. During a rare heart-to-heart conversation over the Christmas period in 1987, as they shared a marijuana joint on a late-night walk near their parents' home in Bellevue, Washington State, Randy told his brother about the abuse. Kevin responded: "I'd no idea."

When asked by *The Mail* to comment on Randy's allegations, a spokesman for Spacey said: "Kevin's brother's claim against his father is a very serious one and has been a difficult personal family matter. The family all feel deeply for his situation. Kevin has not experienced any of the distress that his brother describes as he has never been a victim of abuse and can only sympathise with him."[38] In his biography, Randy observes:

> "Our treatment as children is the real reason why two siblings from the same gene pool, raised in the same basic environment, turned out so different. I was abused, molested and sodomized, while Kevin was nurtured, protected and loved. He was given the tools he needed to conquer the world, and those tools were withheld from me."[39]

Why did Spacey himself not suffer a similar fate to his brother? There appear to have been three main reasons. In December 1971, when Kevin was twelve-and-a-half, Geoff developed an ocular illness for which he was hospitalised. He returned home several weeks later, weakened and looking twenty years older, and never fully recovered his health.[40]

And then there was Kathleen, who adored her youngest son and remained exceptionally close to him throughout her life. She seldom challenged Geoff on any issue, passively accepting his decisions about where the family should live, work, study and go on vacation, but where Kevin was concerned, Mama knew best.

"If you run across the perfume that your mother used, that's a comforting smell," Spacey told *Maxim* in 2001, in an unusually intimate disclosure. "I remember putting my head in my mother's lap when I was young and she used to scratch my head–and I can literally go right back if I smell that particular perfume. It's very comforting, because there was something incredibly secure about my mother scratching my head, making me feel connected to her."[41]

Whether Kathleen was aware of–or suspected–her husband's perverse leanings will never be known. Randy's biography gives a chilling account of the first time his father sexually assaulted his twelve-year-old self in the summer of 1968, after summoning him to the master bedroom to "talk about the birds and the bees." When Kathleen banged on the door in response to Randy's call for help, Geoff ordered him not to respond:

> "Mother came right up. But Father had locked the bedroom door, so she couldn't get in and couldn't see what was happening. She knocked, demanding to know what was going on. I wanted to answer but my father whispered to be quiet. To my surprise, all of a sudden the pounding stopped and there was silence as Mother went back to whatever she'd been doing. I'd never felt so abandoned…My mother did come back, after he was finished and the door was unlocked, to ask what had been going on. Father had told me to tell Mother we had just been talking in private, so that's what I said. I was afraid of what he might do to me if I disobeyed."[42]

On the many occasions that her elder son later tried to discuss the subject with her, Kathleen (whose own unhappy childhood, as noted above, had taught her how to block out anything unpleasant), rejected his pleas with a curt "I don't want to talk about it."[43] Had she been aware, however, she would certainly have taken steps to ensure that her precious Kevin was not victimised too.

Finally, Randy himself has stated that he submitted to Geoff in the hope of keeping him away from his younger brother. "One day when The Creature was screaming "Randall, Randall," preparing to sodomise me, I took his old German Luger and loaded it and sat in the closet, pointing it at my mouth," Randy recounted in *The Mail on Sunday*. "Then I realised if I checked out, there would be nothing to prevent The Creature from forcing my kid brother to take my place. I truly believed when we were growing up that I had succeeded in protecting Kevin."[44] Given this, the fact the siblings have barely spoken since the *Mail* article was published seems especially tragic.

# Chapter Two
# The Boy Who Would Be Spacey

*"Your bio says you were kicked out of school and mentions this tree house incident…"*
*"This is the first thing you learn: if you say it once, it gets repeated and then it*
*actually expands. I read things that I was a bad kid and I was this terror."*
–Kevin Spacey (2001)[45]

*"I can't believe you really went there. I picture you f\*\*\*ing up all*
*the time and making everyone mad and leading mutinies."*
–Actress and former classmate Mare Winningham to Kevin
Spacey re: his time at military school (1997)[46]

Check any potted profile of Kevin Spacey, and it will invariably make
mention of "the tree house incident," in which the rebellious young boy,
playing around with matches, sets a small structure in the garden ablaze. It
has since become part of Spacey lore, referenced in nearly every interview:
sometimes the structure is a tree house, sometimes a doll's house, sometimes
a shed. In all versions of the story, however, Kevin is sent to military school
by his exasperated parents in an attempt to curb his wayward behaviour;
he is later expelled for hurling a tyre at a classmate during a boxing match
and referred to a guidance counsellor, who recommends that the lad's
excess energy might be better deployed into acting classes. A star is born.[47]

The truth appears to be rather more prosaic. The "tree house" was in
reality a chicken coop behind one of the many family rentals where sister
Julie kept a few birds. It was elder brother Randy, while trying to build a
fire to keep the chicks warm, who accidentally set it alight. None of the

birds were harmed in the small conflagration, but the roof of the coop was damaged and they had to be given away.[48]

In August 1969, after several similar transgressions, Randy was sent to Ridgewood Military Academy in Woodland Hills for a short time. While at Ridgewood, Randy was involved in a scuffle with another student who had insulted the girl he invited to their Christmas dance. He threw a desk at the boy, breaking his leg, for which he was put on probation for the rest of the semester–this incident appears to have formed the basis for Spacey's own "schoolboy fight" story.[49] Subsequently, in September 1971, Geoff and Kathleen enrolled Randy at Northridge Military Academy, this time together with his younger brother, an excellent student who was rarely in trouble in or out of class–the fact that Kevin later graduated co-valedictorian from high school is testament to this.

"I could understand why my parents would try to whip me into shape with military school, but I never figured out why Kevin ended up there," Randy says. "Maybe it was a status thing, a demonstration they could afford to have two boys in an expensive institution at once. Or maybe they thought a change of pace would do Kevin good by giving him a different outlook. In any case, he wasn't there more than five, six months and was practically invisible the whole time."[50]

Kathleen's 1984 letter states that her sons were sent to Northridge "to give them a chance of being taught the fundamentals of a good classical education [rather than] merely wasting their time by sitting in a public schoolroom where the teachers have only enough time for discipline and very little left over for teaching." She added: "This was done because we thought it best for Randall and Kevin. Never at any time did either of the boys state they disliked it for any reason, military or otherwise."[51]

Neither sibling was expelled: in March 1972, the Academy was forced to close down due to a lack of funds.[52] As for the counsellor-recommending-acting-classes part of the story, this may well be factually correct, but without the "arson and military expulsion" backup it somehow seems less compelling.

As Randy notes: "To feel complete, [Kevin] has to reshape his own bright, carefree youth into something darker, to make himself more interesting and mysterious."[53] Many a "bad boy" has found refuge in the dramatic arts as an alternative to reform school–Marlon Brando, Steve

McQueen, James Dean, Jack Nicholson and Robert De Niro to name just a few—but the young Kevin Spacey, model pupil, was not among them.

Kevin, it seems, has quite a penchant for "romanticising" such events and using them to enhance his own past. In September 2004, to coincide with the premiere of the first production under his artistic directorship at the Old Vic, he wrote an article for *Condé Nast Traveller* in which he claimed:

> "I first came to London as a child, when my family stayed at a small bed-and-breakfast called the Gower House in central London. One morning, I sat in the window of its breakfast room looking out across the street at a five-story Georgian building buzzing with activity. My mother told me that this was the Royal Academy of Dramatic Art, one of the world's great acting schools…I was captivated by the young actors and actresses mingling outside, smoking cigarettes and looking mysterious, and though I was only eight years old, I already knew I wanted to be one of them.
>
> After we three children came along, my parents saved up their pennies to introduce us to this faraway world, and our family trips to Britain began when I was about six…My parents also had a love of the theater, and they began to take the three of us to plays at a very young age. I know that on one of our trips we saw a production at the Old Vic, but I cannot recall what it was."[54]

The fact that Kevin "cannot recall" which show his younger self saw at the Old Vic is hardly surprising. When Kevin was six, rather than experiencing his "first visit" to Britain, his porn-obsessed father took the family on a very different vacation: a two-week stay at a Los Angeles nudist colony.[55]

Randy remembers visiting London (and England) with Geoff and Kathleen only once, in December 1973, when his brother would have been fourteen-and-a-half. Sister Julie, who embarked on an extended trip to Europe after graduating high school, had recently married Ian Keir, a former amateur football player for the Kilwinning Rangers, and set up home with him in Saltcoats, near Glasgow. The Fowlers–the "Longshore" element of their name had finally been legally jettisoned in July 1971– spent a week sightseeing in London before travelling up to Scotland to see Julie's new abode.[56]

While in the capital the family (who "trooped to a succession of plays"[57] during their stay) appear to have attended a performance at the Aldwych Theatre that featured Tim Pigott-Smith, who would co-star with Spacey in *The Iceman Cometh* some twenty-five years later. "In 1973, I was playing Dr. Watson in an RSC production of Sherlock Holmes," Pigott-Smith stated in a 2001 interview. "One night a huge piece of scenery fell down, smashing furniture and missing me by inches. I called for my butler, who came on and said, 'It's a trifle windy out tonight!' and I said, 'Yes, I should never have moved to Kensington!'

"We got some big laughs and then carried on with the show. Anyway, years later Kevin's in the dressing room [at the Almeida Theatre] telling someone that as a teenager his parents had brought him to London on holiday. He was in the audience that night, and ran through all the ad-libs I'd said on stage. When he finished, I turned round and said, 'Top marks, Kevin, you got that dead right. I was that actor.' He couldn't believe it!"[58] For this anecdote, at least the dates seem to fit.

Perhaps we shouldn't blame Kevin for spinning a few tales for the Press–embellishing one's early life is stock-in-trade for an actor, after all. Some critics chose to see his Old Vic appointment as little more than a publicity stunt, reflecting the current vogue for big Hollywood stars to make well-promoted appearances on the stage for a fraction of their normal pay (despite the fact that Kevin had already financially supported the theatre, which receives no public subsidy, for many years).[59]

So what better way to appease his detractors than with the heart-warming story of a wide-eyed tyke's first glance at the legendary building? "I was so young I don't remember specific productions as much as I remember the spectacle of it and the pageantry of it and how it was such an amazing and beautiful theater,"[60] Spacey told *Time Magazine* in 2003, during a fundraising campaign to fix the Old Vic's leaky roof. He appears to have first contrived the story in August 2000, after investing a six-figure sum in the Old Vic's new share scheme. A *Sunday Times* article from this period noted that "Kevin Spacey, in town to promote the deal, still remembers his first visit to the theatre as a five-year-old in the company of his itinerant parents." "I went to lots of Old Vic productions,"[61] Kevin added.

Even if his December 1973 trip did include a visit to this particular venue, saying he was a spotty adolescent at the time wouldn't make such good copy (or raise as many donations, perhaps). As Spacey-as-Bobby Darin remarks in *Beyond the Sea* (2004): "Memories are like moonbeams. We do with them what we want."[62]

However Kevin got into acting classes, they proved vital in setting him on the path that would eventually lead to Oscar and Tony glory. Although seemingly a "shy" child–he related in a 2002 interview that "up until about the time I was 14, I was very much living in my own world and feeling like I was in my own world. I was sort of, you know, terrified and not very sociable"[63]–little Kevin showed a talent for both drama and music from an early age, giving piano recitals, vocally impersonating celebrities and "staging" crashes on his bicycle for his brother to photograph.[64] "I was always the performer in my house," he said in 2003. "I loved to tell jokes, be silly, and make my mom and dad laugh."[65]

"I started to perform [publicly] in junior high school," Spacey added in 2007. "The first thing I had to do was a pantomime to music. So there was no dialogue. And I created a pantomime to the recording of the theme of *Deliverance*. I created a bank robbery on horseback. I used a chair as a horse, and I remember I fell off it and everybody laughed. When I got to the end of it, I did something that also made them laugh, and they burst into applause. Literally, I was like a dog that hears a whistle that no one else can hear, and I perked up: What is that?"[66]

Kevin briefly considered forming a musical act, to be called Fowler and Company, with his elder sibling. He would be a singing, dancing front man, sometimes doubling on piano, Randy would play the drums, and other musicians would be found to play bass, horns and keyboards. This idea, however, never got past the initial planning stages. By April 1976, at age sixteen, Kevin was already hinting where his real ambition lay. After

Randy took some promotional photos of him dressed up in fencing attire, the youngster enthusiastically scribbled on one:

> "To Randy, I guess after all [our] years of fighting we have finally settled down and got to work together! "Fowler and Company" is going to be hot, it has to be!! I'll invite you to the Academy Awards when I go! Your idol and brother, Kevin Spacey Fowler."[67]

After leaving Northridge Academy, the Fowler brothers finished up at Canoga Park High, where Kevin became more seriously involved with theatrics. As he recounted in 1999:

> "I was in the 11th grade. We performed Arthur Miller's *All My Sons* for the Drama Teachers Association of Southern California. Something happened as I walked off the stage that had never happened to me before. The audience applauded me in the middle of the play. It was the first time I realized I had an effect on people. It was puzzling, confusing, slightly frightening, and it was liberating. Finally acting gave me something to focus on, something I enjoyed that offered me a chance to go into different worlds. All these imaginary games that you played with your friends in the neighborhood–I didn't have to put those games away. I just kept playing them onstage."[68]

That same weekend, the aspiring young thespian attended a production of *The Prime of Miss Jean Brodie* at nearby Chatsworth School in which fellow future stars Mare Winningham and Val Kilmer were performing. After speaking to their drama teacher, Robert Carrelli, Kevin arranged to transfer to Chatsworth himself and later became friendly with both Val and Mare. He has said of Carrelli that "He was a person who gave me a sense of confidence, took an interest and gave me hope. He grabbed me by the scruff of the neck when I most needed it and led me down a different road. I was like many kids in that if my parents made a suggestion, I would turn against it because it was them making it. But with Mr. Carrelli it was different."[69]

"It wasn't until I found theatre," Kevin noted in 2002, "that I found a place where I suddenly felt, 'Wow! I can be myself here.' It was a different kind of environment; it was a different kind of feeling...At the age of 14 or 15 years old, having moved around your whole life, everything was sort of like, suddenly discovering Tennessee Williams, or Eugene O'Neill, or William Shakespeare. Suddenly finding somebody who wrote about family, who wrote about things that I felt I understood. That was quite a startling and exciting moment."[70] In her 1984 letter to her three children, his mother Kathleen references her youngest son's growing involvement in his future career:

> "In high school, there was scarcely a day that he did not need to be driven somewhere [for rehearsals and performances], sometimes as far away as Sunland or Burbank. We never said "no." After he had his driving licence he used my VW more than I did. He never had to take a job to pay for his car insurance or gasoline or pay board and room as so many children did. Why? Because we love him and wanted to make his life as easy as possible."[71]

Kevin appeared in his first Shakespearean production while at Chatsworth, foreshadowing his future collection of wily villains with *Othello's* devious master-manipulator Iago, a Renaissance-era Keyser Söze: his performance won him a top award at a drama competition between seventy-three Los Angeles high schools. "When I was in my teens I was focusing on directing plays and getting up onstage," he said in 2001. "I didn't understand what my friends were going through. I wasn't smoking pot or drinking. I didn't go through those years till I got to New York."[72]

A fan of old Hollywood movies, the young Californian made occasional visits to the Woodland Hills Moving Picture Residential Home, sometimes accompanied by his uncle, former radio announcer Stan "The Dude" Marston (1913-81). Stan, who was married to Kathleen's half-sister Jane, lived with his wife–by then retired from the music business and working as a hair stylist at a Los Angeles beauty salon–in nearby Palo Alto, and maintained a close relationship with his nephew.

Woodland Hills's residents included former Tarzan Johnny Weissmuller–who liked to run around the grounds naked–and two of the original Three Stooges. "Norma Shearer clutched my hand and asked if I was her long-departed husband, the movie mogul Irving Thalberg…"[73] Kevin once claimed. He also enjoyed art house films, once cutting class to attend a showing of Peter Brook's 1971 classic *King Lear* at the rundown NuArt Theater on Santa Monica Boulevard.

Stage and screen great Katharine Hepburn was another one of the teenager's idols. Impressed by a Hepburn performance he attended at the Ahmanson Theatre (*A Matter of Gravity*, which also featured future *Superman* Christopher Reeve), Kevin discovered where she had parked her car and waited patiently beside it after the show to present her with a bouquet of roses. "Hepburn came out a side door, stopped and said, 'You waited for me. How lovely.' She took the roses and sat on the bumper of her car and talked to me for 10 minutes about Spencer Tracy and acting," he recalled in 1999.

Over a decade after their initial encounter, Hepburn was in the Broadway audience for the Spacey play *Long Day's Journey Into Night* and made her way backstage after the performance to congratulate the company. "She walked into the dressing room…hit me on the shoulder and said, 'You must be exhausted!'" Spacey said. "I couldn't bring myself to tell her that I met her as a boy. So the next day I sent her a big bouquet of flowers and a letter explaining to her that we had met once before. She wrote me back a very sweet letter and said it was the first time she had gotten flowers for coming to see a play rather than being in one."[74]

Hepburn subsequently began a correspondence with the young actor that lasted until her own death in 2003. Spacey later related how the long letters detailing his latest achievements were generally met with a terse, polite reply to the effect of: "Dear Kevin, Good for you. Kate."[75]

Kevin graduated from Chatsworth in July 1977 and appeared in the school's farewell show the following month, playing Captain Von Trapp in *The Sound of Music* alongside Mare Winningham as Maria.[76] "[It] was the first time I saw Kevin perform on stage," Randy says. "I came away from the theater that night thinking, 'Wow, my brother's really good.' Even then, I thought he would probably become a superstar in time. He was so into acting, he never had a girlfriend or even a date all through high school."[77]

However, the youngest Fowler sibling suffered a setback shortly afterwards when auditioning his stand-up act for popular TV variety programme *The Gong Show*. He was rejected, or "pre-gonged" (Mare, who also auditioned for the show as a singer/guitarist, got through the qualifying stages and went on to win her round).

While Spacey had contemplated becoming a professional comic and entered himself into several "midnight talent" contests, typically held in bowling alleys full of disinterested patrons ("when all you can hear is the sound of pins being knocked over, it's not very encouraging..."),[78] the *Gong Show* episode appears to have dissuaded him from pursuing this vocation any further. "Comedy," he observed in 2002, "is an incredibly dangerous, terrifying and potentially embarrassing experience. Standing up there and doing what you thought was your best material and...nothing."[79]

"When it works, there's no greater joy...[but] I wouldn't have wanted to do it for a living. It was too brutal,"[80] Kevin noted in another interview. Ironically, he later played a washed-up comic in the film *Rocket Gibraltar* (1988), and has twice hosted variety show *Saturday Night Live*. In one memorable *Star Wars* themed skit, Spacey showed off his flair for parody by imitating Christopher Walken auditioning for the part of Han Solo (in the opinion of the actor's wife Georgianne the "best take off" of her husband ever), Walter Matthau for Obi Wan Kenobi and Jack Lemmon for Chewbacca.[81]

The young Spacey found that his impersonation skills came in useful in other situations too. In December 1977, Randy, forging a career in the music industry as a drummer and instructor, enlisted his brother's help to move into a new apartment in Lake County. While transporting his possessions in Kevin's rusty old car, which had a fake police radio inside, the siblings spotted an abandoned house that had already been broken into several times but still had some interior panelling intact.

Stripping the panelling with an intention to use it in his new home, Randy noticed several people in the neighbouring houses watching them. Worried that someone would alert the authorities, he turned to Kevin, who used the fake radio—and his talent for mimicry—to fool the witnesses into thinking he was a policeman. The brothers got away—with the panelling.[82]

# Chapter Three
# Spacey for Hire

*"When I was 17 I went to a psychic who said I would travel to an island, I would be surrounded by music and then would leave the music and start my life…I thought, OK, take another Quaalude. But a year and a half later I travelled to the island of Manhattan, went to the Juilliard [School of Drama], where the drama department is literally surrounded by the Juilliard School of Music, stayed two years and then left and started my life."*
–Kevin Spacey (1998)[83]

*"Kevin knew he was going to be a big star. And he had no patience to wait for it to happen–he was just going to do whatever he could to be part of that world…"*
–*Independence Day* producer and long-time friend Dean Devlin (1999)[84]

By 1978, the former Kevin Fowler Longshore had become simply Kevin Spacey. He described his decision to amend his name in a 1999 interview as follows:

> "My name has always been Spacey. I was born Kevin Spacey Fowler. Spacey was my middle name. When I was in high school, my grandfather passed away. His last name was Spacey, same as my great grandfather and great uncle. I decided to adopt their name because I missed my grandpa."[85]

As already discussed, it is possible that Kevin's birth name was actually "Kevin Matthew," with the "Spacey" element being added at some later date. The misconception that "Spacey" was Kathleen's maiden name appears to have come from Kevin's assertion that his *grandfather's* last name was Spacey[86]: this cannot have been the case and he seems to have got his generations mixed up. Additionally, by the time Kevin started high school in 1974, paternal grandmother Norma was his only grandparent still living.

Norma and Willard Longshore moved to Calgary in Alberta, Canada–where Willard was engaged by the Stanolind Oil Company–in 1948. Thereafter, Geoff Fowler maintained contact with his mother mostly through correspondence–she disapproved of his political allegiances and reproached him for including hate literature in his letters to her.[87]

Ironically, it is unlikely that Norma ever even met the grandson who has made her family name famous across the globe. Kathleen's 1984 letter mentions that the Longshores visited her and Geoff only once after their marriage, and that Norma belatedly started sending $25 Christmas gifts to her three Fowler grandchildren in the mid-1970s after having had no communication with them previously.[88] Randy has also confirmed that he cannot recall any other contact with Norma, Willard, Allen, Harriet or the long-absent Bayard–whose own 1966 obituary incorrectly recorded that he was survived by his son Thomas "of Canada."[89]

Elsewhere, Kevin described his "mother's father" (this would have to be Allen Knutson, evidently a charmer when sober) in almost mythic terms: "He was the sheriff of a town. One of those raconteur types."[90] Thomas Oscar Spacy of Tennessee (1876-1925), Norma's father and therefore Kevin's great-grandfather, appears to be the only member of the family that actually fits this description: the 1910 United States Federal Census shows his occupation as "Deputy Sheriff," though he is listed as a barber in 1900 and had become a general clerk by 1920!

However it came about–Randy had also suggested that his young brother drop the "Fowler" part of his name–K.F.L. was now K.S., permanently. Following graduation, he attended Los Angeles Valley College and took a typical teen employment route, clearing tables in restaurants (he was once fired "for being the kind of waiter who wouldn't pick up the hot plates"),[91] serving in a shoe shop and selling cable subscriptions door-to-door. His first paid acting job was a shopping centre production of *Romeo and Juliet*, "the best Shakespeare performed in a mall ever,"[92] as Spacey claimed in 2000.

For his participation in this rather unconventional version of the world's most famous romantic play, Kevin received $25. He was also employed for a short while at the Busch Gardens Park in Van Nuys (where his mother was doing secretarial work), tap dancing in one of the revue shows. After his apparently-ascetic high school days, Spacey briefly dated April Winchell, daughter of voice artist Paul, who appeared with him in a summer stock revival of the musical *Gypsy*.

The youngster spent much of his spare time at his brother's flourishing music studio, entertaining Randy's colleagues and students with his dead-on impersonations of *Wild Wild West* star Robert Conrad (who had seen him perform in *The Sound of Music* after accepting an invitation to the play) and talk show legend Johnny Carson.[93] Spacey, who attended recordings of *The Tonight Show* in order to perfect his impression and even obtained the master's autograph on a copy of *Life* magazine, later employed his Carson persona–he pretended to be the host's "son" Kevin– to get himself and friend Dean Devlin into the exclusive New York club Studio 54.

"That's why it was so much fun to party with him," Devlin said in 1999. "Because you always knew Kevin would lead you into some cool adventure. He would just figure out a way to maximize the experience."[94] "I guess I abused it, but hey, when you've got no money…you do what you can,"[95] Spacey admitted in a 2003 interview.

Young Kevin also liked to infiltrate the studio backlots of Universal, Fox, Paramount and Warner Brothers. "I would put a hammer on the side of my belt and just walk in with a group of people and wave. I'd wander around and very often get asked to help someone do something," he recalled in 1999. Hefting furniture across soundstages seemed a fair trade-off for the chance to watch television shows–such as a *Kojak* episode with Telly Savalas–being filmed. "It was dangerous and fun," Spacey added. "It was like, 'Some day I'm gonna …'"[96]

"Some day" soon came. At the urging of his friend Val Kilmer, who was already a student there, in the summer of 1979 Kevin auditioned for the prestigious Juilliard Performing Arts School in Manhattan, using an extract from *Othello*. Drama Division director Michael Langham, failing to recognise the Shakespearian piece, asked if he had written his own monologue, whilst vocal coach Elizabeth Smith told him he was interesting, "but your voice sounds like the end of a frayed rope."[97]

Despite this unpromising start, Kevin became one of only 28 students accepted into Juilliard's 1979 acting programme, borrowing money for his tuition fees from Val's wealthy father, Eugene. "[Kevin] was chosen out of the whole student body, because we were one male short for a Chekhov play, early *Uncle Vanya*, and he played my father, and he knew my father, and it was pretty scary how well he played him,"[98] Kilmer has said. The two later fell out after Kilmer claimed that Kevin had never paid Eugene back[99] (Val on Kevin: "He's just lucked out, and he's full of subterfuges, among other things"; Kevin on Val: "I wouldn't *think* to do the kinds of projects or roles he does.")[100]

The pair appear to have settled their differences in recent years. When Kilmer came to London in 2005 to star in *The Postman Always Rings Twice* at the Playhouse Theatre they were spotted dining together at The Ivy restaurant, and Spacey also attended his former classmate's birthday party, held at Val's River Thames-side apartment. "[Kevin] called me up to wish me luck," said Val. "And I apologised in advance for the fact that nobody will be going to see his new production [at the Old Vic] because they will all be at my show"[101] (Kilmer, incidentally, was wrong: *Postman* was a flop).

After completing two years of the four-year Juilliard acting course (fellow students included Kelly McGillis, Elizabeth McGovern and Ving Rhames), young Kevin found that many of his classes were becoming tedious and unproductive. He stopped attending them, preferring to spend his time in impromptu play rehearsals rather than sitting through dreary lectures on the intricacies of Elizabethan language or the history of American theatre.

"I had a teacher at Juilliard [Elizabeth Smith] that was incredible, who I presumed didn't care for me because she was so tough on me," he noted in 2002. "I said that one day in sort of heated anger about some confrontation that we had. She said to me, 'You big *idiot!*' She said, 'Don't you realize that I'm hard on you because I think and I know that you're the most talented student in this class and the *laziest.*' And I was, like 'whoa!' I think people drop seeds, and sometimes it took a while for those seeds to grow…"[102]

"I think what [the teachers] tended to do," Kevin mused in 2007, "was in some sense decide, in whatever way they did, what kind of actor you were going to be, and they wanted to strip you, in some degree, of your personality. To turn you into a kind of neutral figure and then build on that."[103] It is perhaps telling that the only drama workshop where Spacey felt truly at ease was one in which he was required to conceal his face: "You put on a mask and suddenly you don't see you. It makes you comfortable. You find your body doing things you usually wouldn't. It's about being able to invent yourself each time out."[104]

Having decided that he had absorbed all the knowledge Juilliard had to offer, Kevin dropped out in mid-1981:

> "I left about four days before they would have asked me to leave...I made up the rules. I changed the game. It wasn't that I wasn't doing my work, but I wasn't willing to sit in classes that I didn't feel were helping me. My ambition was fierce and I was selfish. It took me a while to figure out my responsibility as an actor and to understand what it means to work with a group of people in a company. Still, through a lot of diligent phone calling and harassing, I got myself an audition for Shakespeare in the Park and got in. Val also got in at that time. We were in *Henry VI, Part I* in inconsequential parts, but we were getting paid $125 a week to do Shakespeare for [producer and founder] Joe Papp, which is the greatest fucking dream for an actor.
>
> I thought I was all set, but then I couldn't get arrested. It's hard to get auditions, harder to get scripts. I went back to Joe and gave him my sad song, and he hired me to work in the stockroom [at the Public Theater]. I was there for three months. I eventually worked my way up to Papp's office, which was how I ended up getting to know him. We became friends."[105]

Spacey later credited Papp for his part in inspiring him to become a crusader for the arts. "There will never be anyone like Joe, a true fighter for the theatre," he said in 2000. "I remember the day in 1982 when they knocked down two theatres in New York that Joe had campaigned to save, to build a hotel. I vowed then that if there was ever a time when I could pick up Joe's mantle, I would do the same."[106]

While Spacey was working in Papp's office, he also appeared in a small off-off-Broadway Dance Space production of Friedrich Schiller's 1781 play *The Robbers* on 13th Street. In the lead role of charismatic outlaw Karl Moor, Kevin reportedly received a review in *The Village Voice* that compared him favourably to both Marlon Brando and frequent Brando collaborator Karl Malden ("For weeks my friends called me 'Marlon Malden,'"[107] he quipped in 1999). To publicise the play, Kevin had business cards printed announcing that "Kevin Spacey cordially invites you to *The Robbers*."[108] One found its way onto Papp's desk, prompting the producer to attend a performance.

The day after seeing the show, Papp fired Kevin from his $125-a-week office job, telling him: "I saw an actor onstage last night, and that's what you should be doing. You're becoming too secure working here. You need to get out and act."[109] Spacey, now forced to focus on performing full-time, has described his early years in New York in almost Dickensian terms:

> "I was terrified. I had no job, no rent money. I was living in a building where I was the super, sweeping the halls and taking out the trash so they would cut my rent."[110]

The extent of his penury during those days, however, may have been exaggerated. Randy claims that Kevin's tale[111] of cashing in aluminium cans in order to buy food for himself–and his dog, Slaight, a large black Labrador that Spacey adopted after finding the abandoned animal tied to a pole in the East Side district in 1981–is another incident from his own life that his brother has appropriated.

By Randy's account, Kathleen continued to support her younger son financially, ensuring that he always had enough cash to pay his rent and food bills–her 1984 letter states that "we sent him money for a long period of time, as we could afford it and were happy to be able to do it."[112] "[Kevin] never wanted for anything," Randy says. "Look at his pictures from the time he talks about–he doesn't appear to have missed a meal."[113]

Spacey also had income from a rather unusual source. On 27th July 1981–the day after Kevin's twenty-second birthday–Norma Spacy Fowler

Longshore died in Canada. Norma's obituary in *The Calgary Herald* noted that "she is remembered for her musical services which she provided as an organist at Calgary churches,"[114] and that she was survived by four children, eight grandchildren and one great-granddaughter (Julie's daughter Ingrid).

A month before her death, Norma had changed her will to exclude her eldest son and Geoff's share of her estate–several oil wells in Calgary that she had inherited from Willard, who predeceased her in 1969–produced royalties that were split between Julie, Randy and Kevin. They received modest cheques every few months for several years, until the oil wells dried up.[115]

In any case, the roles came thick and fast, even if they paid little (and involved a lot of travelling). In order to find a wider choice of parts with which to advance his craft, the young actor made regular trips across the U.S. and appeared in several regional stage productions including *The Mousetrap* in Virginia, *Sleuth* in New Jersey and *Real Dreams* in Williamstown, Massachusetts. In 1981, he spent a few months teaching weekend acting classes at St Thomas's Episcopal Church in Mamaroneck, New York, to students from ages eleven up to eighteen.

Spacey made his Broadway debut–and gained his Equity card–in 1982, playing syphilitic bohemian son Oswald in *Ghosts*, Henrik Ibsen's 1881-penned caustic comment on nineteenth-century social mores. *Ghosts*, which also featured Liv Ullmann and John Neville, opened at the Eisenhower Theater in Washington D.C. on 2nd August and ran for 24 performances before transferring to the Brooks Atkinson Theater in New York. Geoff and Kathleen Fowler travelled from their home in Hayden Lake, Idaho, where they had relocated in 1981, to watch an early showing in Washington D.C., while Joseph Papp and his wife Gail attended the New York premiere.

Spacey received some positive notices for his performance–described as "unusually effective"[116] by one local paper–though many other viewers remained unimpressed. *The New York Times's* review of the show's opening night on Broadway noted: "As the son, Kevin Spacey accents one note, youthful ardor, and never convinces us that he has artistic inclinations or a terminal illness."[117] *The Capital's* Jay Sharbutt was even more dismissive: "All is undone by clashing accents, alternately melodramatic or static staging, and unconvincing acting by the supporting cast, particularly Kevin Spacey, mawkish as the widow's doomed artist son."[118]

Kevin—who once claimed to have been "the worst Oswald in history"[119]— later confirmed that he was unhappy at this point in his professional life:

> "I truly sucked. I was miserable, working out of fear. I became a bit of a jerk. It's a period in my life I'm not proud of. It cost me friendships. I wasn't good enough and it was a hard thing to admit. I had all this talent inside, but it was undeveloped and raw, untried and unfocused. I was inexperienced and yet I had this huge ambition…I was behaving in a way that I now find reprehensible. It took me a couple of years to really shake that off and say, 'That's not the life I want to live.'"[120]

> "From 1982 to 1984, I just didn't sleep. I could not fucking relax! I would just stay up, coming up with plans how I was gonna make it, writing this really depressing shit in my diary, or comparing myself to people I knew who were doing well. The worst part is, even when I got work in regional theater in Williamstown or Seattle, I'd come back to town and I wouldn't have an apartment anymore. Talk about a living hell! It's, like, summer in New York, the humidity's 900 percent, and I'm banging on friends' doors asking them if I can stay on their couch. 'And by the way, would you mind if my ninety-pound Labrador comes too?' I mean, that's desperation. That is the fucking definition of desperation."[121]

One of the friends whose door Spacey "banged on" was Sarah St. George, the daughter of multi-millionaire racehorse owner and industrialist Edward St. George. "I knew him for about three months when he stayed with me in New York. He was incredibly fun and a nice friend," St. George told *The Observer's* David Smith in 2004.

"Kevin was always determined to become an actor. Every day he was going to auditions all the time, but it took him a long time to get going. He was a bit despondent. He wasn't earning very much money and it was hard to make a living. He always had friends he stayed with. It was a close-knit community and everybody looked after everybody else...He was a professional and a bit of a loner when I knew him."[122]

St. George, who also confirmed that "I haven't heard from Kevin for 25 years," was incorrectly described in another publication as one of his closest friends, "almost like Kevin's sister."[123] "Such is the Spacey mythology," David Smith noted after speaking to St. George, "half of everything written about him is probably untrue."[124]

Spacey continued to seek out roles in the theatre, having decided during his Juilliard years that he would avoid auditioning for overtly commercial roles in TV ads or soap operas. As he stated in 1992: "In the end, you are the only person who can maintain your integrity. You get offered a lot of things when you are starting out. But it's a little like losing your virginity. Once you lose it, it's gone for good."[125] He later overcame his aversion to commercials, becoming the U.S. "voice of Honda" in 2005 and appearing as himself in U.K. ads for both American Airlines ("you'll know when you find the right seat") and Olympus cameras ("don't be a tourist") in 2009.

Whilst working for the Seattle Repertory Company in January 1984 (he appeared in Shakespeare's *As You Like It* and Molière's *The Misanthrope*), Kevin received a call from Randy, then on his way to a band audition in Portland. Despite their closeness as children and young adults, the siblings had lost touch with one other after both left California, Kevin for Juilliard and the East Coast stage and Randy to go on the road with several different music groups across the United States. Randy asked his brother for a $150 loan; Spacey agreed to send him $50.[126]

It was to be their last conversation for over three more years, though Kevin did post his sibling an autographed headshot with this encouraging message a few months later: "Dear Randy, No matter what, stay on that stage. Never give up an honest lover! With warmth from your brother, Kevin Spacey." Spacey attached a copy of a business card with his agent's details to the photo, circling the phone number with a felt-tip pen, indicating that Randy would need to contact him via "official" channels in the future.[127]

Randy soon found a new loan source. In October 1985, mother Kathleen–playing her regular stake of 1, 4, 8, 11, 14, and 23, numbers that had reputedly been gifted to her in childhood by a mysterious elderly woman who had approached the young girl in the street with the information and then, fairy godmother-like, vanished from sight–won the Washington LOTTO pool of $1.7 million, payable in yearly instalments of $69,449.68 over the next twenty years.[128] Spacey, meanwhile, was about to hit his own theatrical jackpot.

# Chapter Four

# Spacey's Journey

*"I think you have a massive ego—you do. You have a massive ego. But I think it is as healthy as you can get. You are constantly on the alert for your own betterment, but that's what you're supposed to be. Who else is going to do it? To a lesser degree, people who work for you. But basically, it's up to you."*
–Jack Lemmon to Kevin Spacey (2000)[129]

*"Lemmon, my dear, dear Jack…This is a man who was at the top of his profession for 40 years, and he never became a dick. You know?"*
–Kevin Spacey's tribute to Jack Lemmon (2001)[130]

As Kevin learned when he and Randy had raided the abandoned Californian house for panelling, theft can pay dividends–providing you get away with it. In early 1985, Spacey attended a lecture on "The Afterlife of Plays" by the theatrical director and neurologist Dr. Jonathan Miller at his old alma mater, the Juilliard School.[131] Glancing at a well-dressed elderly lady dozing next to him, he noticed an invitation to a post-lecture cocktail reception to "honour" the great man poking out of her handbag. Deciding that the old dear needed her rest, he pilfered the ticket and attended the event in her place.

A favourite anecdote of Kevin's, frequently recounted on talk shows, this may well be another embellished tale. Exactly how he got there, however, is not as important as the result. Spacey sauntered into the function room and, after knocking back a few drinks at the bar, took the seat next to Miller (which had just been vacated by a bathroom-bound Kurt Vonnegut) and described his months of difficulty in trying to get an audition for the director's upcoming production of Eugene O'Neill's *Long Day's Journey Into Night*.

Written around 1940 but unperformed until 1956, three years after its author's death, *Long Day's Journey* won the Pulitzer Prize for Drama in 1957 and is widely considered to be O'Neill's most powerful play. Set in 1912, it covers one fateful, heart-rending day from early morning to midnight at the seaside Connecticut home of the Tyrones–the autobiographical representations of O'Neill himself, his older brother, and their parents. Addiction is a running theme: the three males are alcoholics whilst mother Mary is dependent on morphine, and all four are trapped in a seemingly-inescapable spiral of guilt, conflict, accusation, counter-accusation and denial that worsens as the "journey into night" draws closer: a sad conclusion indeed.

Spacey's own "journey" had a happier ending. Having snagged Miller's telephone number at the cocktail party (much to the chagrin of *Journey's* casting team, who were also in attendance and had already turned Kevin down several times), he was invited to attend the next round of auditions two days later. "I've always related to O'Neill," he noted in 1998. "His father was a successful but artistically failed actor; my father was a technical writer who was a failed novelist."[132]

Miller has recently revealed that he found the actor's approach somewhat unsettling. "He loomed up rather threateningly to me at the reception and asked me why I hadn't put him on the list...I wanted to get rid of him in order to get on with the party." The director was impressed by Spacey's interpretation of the role of eldest child Jamie, however–"I must have been attracted by something about his demeanour"[133]–and Kevin landed the part after legendary actor Jack Lemmon, who played father James Sr. and had the final word on the casting of his "sons," gave his approval.

"I couldn't sleep for weeks in advance," Kevin recounted in 2004. "To act with Jack Lemmon was a terrifying prospect. But I'd been really working and preparing, and we did about four scenes together, very rapid and fast. The relationship is between a father and a son, and the son is very volatile. The way I played him in that audition was kind of relentless. Jack put his hand on my shoulder once we'd finished and said, 'You know what? I never thought I'd find the rotten kid, but you're it.'"[134]

*Journey's* producer Emanuel Azenberg (who later worked with Kevin on *Lost in Yonkers* and the Broadway version of *The Iceman Cometh*) has claimed that Spacey then had "a serious reputation for messing around." The exact nature of this "messing around" has not been revealed, however, in order to secure the role of Jamie, Spacey apparently had to agree to give his "word of honor to be a good citizen."[135]

Working with Jack Lemmon proved a pivotal experience for Spacey. He had first met the actor–briefly–as a young teenager, when his drama class attended a showing of *Juno and the Paycock* at the Mark Taper Forum in Los Angeles that included a workshop session with the stars of the play. After watching Spacey's performance in a group exercise, Lemmon went over to the boy and, as Spacey stated in a 2008 interview with *American Way Magazine*, apparently told him: "You ought to think about becoming an actor. That was terrific. This kid's got talent."[136]

Lemmon also autographed a photo of himself that the young fan had brought along, writing: "With my very best wishes always."[137] When relating the story of their initial encounter in an article he wrote for *AARP Magazine* in 2004, Kevin described it rather differently:

> "I first met Jack when I was a junior high school student. I was about 13 years old. My class had taken a trip to see a production of a Sean O'Casey play called *Juno and the Paycock*, which starred Jack, Walter Matthau, and Maureen Stapleton. They did a Q and A afterward, and I asked Jack for advice: 'What should I do to become an actor?' He looked me directly in the eye and he said, 'If you're really serious about being an actor, then you should go to New York and study theater.' And I did. It was great advice."[138]

Whatever the truth about their first meeting may be, their second saw the start of a firm friendship between established star and gifted newcomer, as Spacey and Lemmon spent a year on the road together performing the play in four separate countries. After initial previews in Durham, North Carolina, and Washington D.C., *Long Day's Journey* premiered at the

Broadhurst Theatre, New York City, on 22nd April 1986. Following its Broadway run, the production transferred to London (possibly Spacey's second visit to the capital) where it opened at the Theatre Royal Haymarket on 4th August.

Spacey was unable to bring Slaight–who once lifted his leg to Lemmon's expensively embroidered golf club bag–all the way from the U.S. Impresario Duncan Weldon, who later co-produced *The Philadelphia Story* for the Old Vic, noted in 2004 that "In *Long Day's Journey* [Kevin] was a totally unknown actor. I do recall he had a dog in France and it couldn't come here because of quarantine. He was so devoted he used to go across to France every weekend, solely because of his dog."[139]

Slaight was later succeeded by Legacy, another black Lab, and Mini, a Jack Russell terrier cross puppy Spacey obtained from Battersea Dogs Home when appearing in the London run of *The Iceman Cometh* (Kevin refers to her as "my British bitch.")[140] Spacey–who was unable to have a dog as a child, as father Geoff preferred cats–clearly adores his pets. He once claimed that his "idea of heaven"[141] would be to walk through the front door and be buried under a pile of dogs as they rushed to greet him. "If you're in hotels–and God knows we are, a lot," he remarked to fellow dog-owner Lemmon in 2000, "it just makes it so great to walk in at the end of the day and get that unconditional love no matter how the day has gone."[142]

In order to give *Journey* a more "naturalistic" feel, Miller shortened its usual four-hour running time to around two hours and forty minutes by overlapping the dialogue at several points. No Tyrone in this version has the courtesy to "wait their turn," even for the most grandiose address. Miller also made some cuts to the text in Act Four: sadly Jamie's final comments on his morphine-addict mother's deteriorating mental health were included in the cull.

Spacey was virtually eliminated from the last scene, losing the opportunity to give his character a significant exit, as was noted in a contemporary American review of the show:

> "His last memorable line in this production is 'The Mad Scene. Enter Ophelia,' which is played mostly for laughs, so that Jamie seems too unaffected by his mother's condition; he is too much the devil-may-care cynic. While Kevin Spacey gives an excellent

performance as Jamie, and even captures flashes of the self-hatred that lies beneath the cynical bitterness (especially in the climactic confessional scene with [brother] Edmund), yet he is denied his proper 'leave-taking,' and thus remains the sneering cynic, rather than the bitter, broken, lost young man he should be at the play's end."[143]

"Self-hatred," "cynical bitterness," "sneering cynic"–these (affected) traits would become Spacey's trademarks during his star-making screen career in the Nineties. O'Neill's detailed character synopsis also emphasises these qualities: Jamie has a "habitual expression of cynicism...on the rare occasions when he smiles without sneering, his personality possesses the remnant of a humorous, romantic, irresponsible Irish charm." His father first introduces him with the words: "He's for ever making sneering fun of somebody, that one."[144]

Not a huge success by Broadway standards–many American critics disapproved of Miller's decision to overlay the speeches and found the truncated play too "fast"–*Long Day's Journey* was much better received in the West End, where it earned excellent notices and became a sell-out smash. Margaret Thatcher, the then-Prime Minister, even attended a performance. "Since I saw this production in New York four months ago, it has gained in richness and force," was *The Sunday Times's* John Peter's verdict. "Kevin Spacey and Peter Gallagher play the two sons not only with an awesome sense of physical detail but also with fearless honesty: they are never afraid to bring out the repugnant side of these characters. This is one of the finest things Miller has ever done..."[145]

"There's this false reverence for *Journey* [in the U.S.] that is so full of shit. It doesn't bring the play any life," Kevin told *Rocket Gibraltar* writer Amos Poe in 1989. "In London they sure appreciated it because they don't have O'Neill on a pedestal; there isn't a designated way to do it. They just thought it was a damn good production."[146]

"There's no question that while I was doing that play, I loved living here [London]; I loved the people," Spacey–who reputedly slept on the floor of Lemmon's room at the Savoy to avoid having to stay in a cheap hostel–added in a 2004 interview. "There was just something incredible about being an American actor and working on the London stage."[147] The production later transferred to Israel and finally, Toronto.

Spacey and Lemmon worked together several times after *Journey*. They appeared as unrelated characters in the TV miniseries *The Murder of Mary Phagan* in 1988,[148] and as father-and-son-in-law in the film *Dad* in 1989. Their last shared theatrical release was 1992's *Glengarry Glen Ross*, David Mamet's savage tale of real-estate sales machinations, with Lemmon playing desperate veteran Shelley Levene and Spacey spiteful office manager John Williamson. It is a measure of the talent of both actors that the gloating contempt Williamson displays towards Levene, who has faked a robbery to pay for his sick daughter's cancelled operation–"Because I–don't–like you!"–at the film's climax is so convincing.

"I didn't even tell Jack when I was auditioning for *Glengarry Glen Ross*," Spacey commented in 2004. "I knew that Jack had flown in for it, and I remember I walked into the room and Jack was sitting there with his script and he looked up and saw me and went, 'Oh, can't you do something on your own?'"[149]

Since Lemmon's death in 2001, Spacey has often referred to the elder actor as being a surrogate parent to him. In a 2008 interview with *The Sunday Times*, Kevin said:

> "I had some really f***ing great mentors in my life, who passed down what in my estimation were some pretty wise ideas. Especially after my father died, Jack Lemmon became a father figure to me. Jack always used to say that if you've done well in the business that you wanted to be in, then it is your obligation to send the elevator back down. That's your job, because somebody did it for you. It's more satisfying than any individual achievement because you can change people's lives."[150]

Lemmon's feelings towards Spacey were equally convivial. In an interview with Miller conducted during *Journey's* long run, Jack noted: "There has never been any experience in my life to equal the sheer joy of being part of this production...not just the material and the character but the people that I'm working with. It is 100% of a fantasy."[151]

Lemmon later wrote a letter of recommendation to help Spacey secure an apartment in New York, stating that he was "an upstanding young man, and to [my] knowledge the only thing [he has] ever stolen [is my] scenes."[152] During his eulogy at Jack's funeral, son Chris named Peter Gallagher, golfer Peter Jacobsen and Kevin himself as "my father's other three sons."[153] Lemmon's directive to "send the elevator back down" became a personal missive of Kevin's, first realised through his production company Trigger Street.

Frustrated by having to mark so many unsolicited scripts "return to sender"–as is generally the policy in the film industry to avoid potential lawsuits–the by-then-world-famous Spacey decided to do something about it. As he stated in 1996, shortly before founding the company: "To me it comes down to this: there is nothing about achieving anything, even an Academy Award, that has any value if you can't share it, if you can't take that and parlay it, use it to help get attention for other people, people who deserve it...I think the idea of power for its own sake is incredibly shallow. The only power that matters is the power to give some new voice the break it wouldn't otherwise get."[154]

"I know what it feels like," he told CNN anchorwoman Connie Chung in 2002, "to have doors slammed in your face and be told you're not good enough, and you're not this enough and you're quirky and you don't quite fit into a mold. I am really happy that there were a lot of people who had faith in me long before I even had it in myself, who gave me a leg up, and I think that the kind of person I am is now trying to sort of give that back, because I don't know what else to do with it."[155]

In November of that year, Spacey and business partner Dana Brunetti launched TriggerStreet.com, an online forum for unrepresented writers and short film directors. As it states on the website: "TriggerStreet is a community of filmmakers, screenwriters, and film aficionados gathered together in the virtual space to share and critique scripts and short films. This community provides a platform for undiscovered talent to showcase their work and gain valuable exposure and feedback that it may not normally have access to. It is also a venue to learn about the art of screenwriting and filmmaking by critiquing others' work."[156]

Users earn "credits" for reviewing the projects of other members and are able to upload their own short films and screenplays onto TriggerStreet. com in return. The highest-ranked films are shown at a yearly festival where the overall winner—who receives a $50,000 cash award—is selected by a panel of industry professionals (past judges have included Sam Mendes, Bryan Singer and Spacey himself), while Trigger Street Productions retains a first-look option on the site's most popular screenplays for ninety days.

Almost uniquely in the film world, there is no charge for the service, which was recently expanded to encompass the submission of comics, plays, short stories and novels. The name "Trigger Street" is a reference to an actual street (named after cowboy star Roy Rogers's famous horse) in Chatsworth, close to where Spacey attended high school and on which pal Val Kilmer lived for a time; perhaps they once staged a bicycle crash there together.

# Chapter Five

# Spacey Rising

*"I wanted to do something so left of center that no one would be able to figure it out..."*
–Kevin Spacey on his role as Mel Profitt in *Wiseguy* (1991)[157]

*"Some days, I don't have a clue as to what I'm going to do. I go out to dinner. I read until one or two in the morning. I don't party. I can't tolerate arrogance. And I have a little dog named Legacy who has the biggest ears you've ever seen."*
–Kevin Spacey's "self-portrait" for *Entertainment Weekly* (1991)[158]

"'Scuse me, would you like to sit down?" A young man with badly tinted orange-blond hair and a small scar down one cheek offers a heavily pregnant Meryl Streep his pew on a crowded train. A closer shot of said young man displays his disconcertingly sneery smile; after he flashes her a quick wink sensible Meryl frowns and folds her hand over her engagement ring. Her suspicions are later justified when the ruffian follows her to a therapy group meeting and puts a gun to her head. He forces the group to surrender their assorted valuables and then makes a swift exit, seemingly a little contrite–"I'm really sorry about your ring, lady," he tells our heroine– never to be seen or heard from again.

So that was *Heartburn* (1986), Kevin Spacey's movie debut. Billed as "Subway Thief" in the credits, he has just six lines of dialogue and about two minutes of screen time. "It was horrifying," he said in 1999. "I couldn't wink [at Meryl]. I was so nervous that my face was twitching."[159]

Kevin was cast in the film by director Mike Nichols, who had worked with him on Broadway in 1984-85 when the actor had understudied *Hurlyburly*, David Rabe's bleakly comic play about a misogynistic, toked-up group of mid-level Hollywood hustlers. Acting coach John Swanbeck, a long-time friend of Spacey's, told an interviewer in 1999 that "As an understudy he carried himself like the leading man...because he knew it was coming. Some people thought he didn't have any right to be so sure, they have often underestimated him, and he has confounded them at every turn."[160]

"Kevin was still in his mid-20s," Nichols concurred, "yet at one point or another, he played every [male] part, which included replacing Bill Hurt, Chris Walken, Harvey Keitel and several others, and each time he played it brilliantly."[161] "They tried to get me to do [female lead] Darlene," Spacey once quipped, "but I wouldn't wear the dress."[162]

"Bill Hurt terrified me, completely terrified me," Kevin later recalled of his *Hurlyburly* days (he also appeared in the film adaptation in 1998). "He was the best actor around–everything I thought an actor should be. He would walk into a room, and I was freaked out by him. I used to sneak into the theater to rehearse because I was an understudy and they never let you rehearse on the stage. You'd have to sneak in.

"I was out there one day, and I looked up and Bill Hurt had walked onto the stage. He'd gotten there early. This is literally what he did to me. Arms folded, he sizes me up. 'My, my, my, what *have* we here? A dedicated *actor?* What *are* you doing?'"[163] "It was a remarkable education, you know," Spacey mused in 2007, "to get up every night on a Broadway stage and do a performance, and nobody knew who I was. I wasn't famous, I was just an actor. And it was one of the best experiences ever just in terms of learning and training and that consistency."[164]

It seems somehow fitting that Spacey made his cinematic debut opposite Streep, widely regarded as the finest actress of the 1980s, as he would be considered the finest actor of the following decade. Kevin's first film role also gave him an opportunity to play tricks on the audience–the polite young man who surrenders his seat to a lady in need actually has an ulterior motive. Like many subsequent Spacey characters, the Subway Thief is not all he seems. Just like his scar...

Ah, the "scar." After his expressive eyes his most distinctive facial feature, the inch-long groove Spacey sports down the right side of his kisser is not a scar at all but a skin wrinkle, a genetic characteristic of the Fowler family: father Geoff had them also. This has not stopped Kevin playfully claiming that he received it "in a duel"–perhaps he was thinking of the fencing pictures that brother Randy took in 1976?

Spacey does have at least three genuine scars, however. The crease above the lid of his left eye is the legacy of a childhood altercation with a cat named Prince Albert,[165] while the dimple on his left cheek results from a cyst that was removed by surgery in the late Eighties after it grew to painful proportions. In *See No Evil, Hear No Evil* (1989), it is particularly prominent. He also bears a small "<" shaped furrow above one eyebrow, the mark left by a cardboard coathanger cover thrown at him by Randy during a spat between the siblings in 1968.

Following his debut in *Heartburn*, Spacey guested on two television drama shows, *The Equalizer* (as a corrupt cop) and *Crime Story* (as a zealous young senator stung by the Mob) and began to work regularly in film. Director Howard Davies and writer Christopher Hampton chose him to replace Alan Rickman in *Les Liaisons Dangereuses* on Broadway–"One morning this geezer walks in, slightly overweight, a bit wild…"[166]–but were thwarted by the show's producers who wanted a more famous actor.

"I didn't care that he was unknown, his audition was brilliant,"[167] Davies (who promptly closed the show in protest at not being allowed to use young Kevin) remarked in 1999. The moneymen were similarly unenthusiastic about the actress Davies and Hampton picked to take over the lead female role: a pre-*Fatal Attraction* Glenn Close.

Kevin was reunited with Mike Nichols for the blockbuster movie *Working Girl* (1988), a part he got by chance when the director fired another actor and needed a replacement on short notice. As sleazy business executive Bob Speck, Spacey has only one scene, though as the first bona fide "classic" movie on his résumé it is worthy of mention. "I had never read the script, so I had no idea what the movie was about until I went and saw it. You could do worse than spend the day snorting coke on Melanie Griffith's lap…"[168] Spacey later mused on his brief role.

Kevin raised some eyebrows when he confessed in a 2001 *Maxim* interview to having had a bad experience with the drug himself "a very long time ago, 1986" (the actor's experimentation with illegal substances is, perhaps, the "messing around" that *Journey's* producer Emanuel Azenberg referred to):

> "[I] just had one of those moments where you think, Oh, this was such a bad idea. I mean, my heart actually kind of did a little flutter and it absolutely terrified me. Of course, a couple of friends dying is the only lesson you need about drugs. And I feel lucky because I'm the kind of personality that if I had gone down that road, down the road of drinking, I'd be sitting on a barstool right now saying, 'It should've been me, it should've been me.' But I stopped. I literally recognised that if I continued to experiment in that fashion I'd be done."[169]

Spacey would soon develop an addiction to heroin–but only on the screen. His first (and to date, last) regular role in a television series, *Wiseguy*, gained him a small cult following that would doubtless have reached epic proportions if the Internet had been in general use at the time. Mel Profitt is an extraordinarily complex character for an action drama from the dumbed-down Eighties, where supporting personnel typically had about as much depth as a July puddle.

*Wiseguy* was produced by Stephen J. Cannell, co-creator of the noisily plotless *A-Team*, and premiered in the fall of September 1987, after the earlier show's cancellation in June of that year. Shot in Vancouver, British Columbia, it concerns the exploits of undercover FBI agent Vinnie Terranova (played by Ken Wahl)–the "Wiseguy" of the title–who infiltrates criminal organisations, gathers enough evidence to destroy them and then moves on.

While Wahl himself gave a generally insipid performance in the lead, the programme was distinguished by a bravura supporting cast that included Ray Sharkey as catlike mobster Sonny Steelgrave and Jonathan Banks as Terranova's droll boss McPike. Kevin joined the cast halfway through the first season: his super-racketeer Profitt becomes Terranova's second target.

A true Renaissance crook, Profitt involves himself in international drug smuggling, arms sales, espionage and prostitution, "the grease that makes the world such a great place to be," as fellow undercover agent

Roger Lococco (William Russ) tells Vinnie. Mel, who considers himself a "Malthusian," keeps a bust of Georgian British economist Thomas Malthus on his luxury yacht and believes the crystal amulet around his neck contains his soul. "The man has an I.Q. of over 200 and he prays to hat racks…" Lococco remarks to his co-employee. "I hope you can figure out who this guy is, because he sure doesn't know," Vinnie scribbles cryptically on a note to McPike after his first meeting with Profitt.

Mel Profitt was another role for which Spacey was a late replacement, the original actor cast in the part having been placed in a rehab centre by his father shortly before filming commenced. Having flown to Los Angeles (where the *Wiseguy* auditions took place) at the urging of his managers and then-agent Kevin Huvane, who wanted their client to "shake some hands out there," Spacey was initially reluctant to put himself forward for a commercial prime-time show:

> "I had steadfastly refused to go to L.A. and knock on doors. It has been the thing that has disinterested me more than anything else. Having grown up there, I knew what it had to offer. And I said, 'Alright, I'll go out, but I'm not going out to look for a job: I'm just going out to meet people. I don't want to audition.' This is one of those great Hollywood stories that you never think's going to happen to you.
>
> I arrive at LAX, I rent a car, [Slaight] in the back seat, drive to William Morris to pick up a couple of scripts that I'm supposed to read before I'm going on to the house that I'm staying at. I'm in the office of one of the agents–I'm talking, I'm chatting–and suddenly the agent says, 'Well, now, what are you doing?' And I said, 'I'm jet lagged, I'm going to go crash for a while.' And she said, 'There's an appointment for something that has just come up, they're kind of in a jam, would you go over?' She told me about it a little bit, and I said, 'Oh, alright, alright, alright.'"[170]

After being offered the part of Mel by a now-desperate production team, Spacey turned it down three times, accepting only after some forceful persuasion by Cannell. "The people there were thinking, Who is this pathetic no-name theater actor who dropped out of the sky saying no? But Steve convinced me. He showed me the story arc. I watched for an hour and was astounded that it wasn't about car chases but about character. I read some scripts and saw that the writing was fantastic."[171] "So that was my trip to L.A.," Spacey later related, "two days. I got [a] job and I was gone: my dog was still in the back seat of the car."[172]

Like many of Spacey's later screen characters—Buddy Ackerman, Jack Vincennes, Lester Burnham—his Profitt is a curious mix of vulnerability and menace. Abandoned in a Dumpster with his infant sister Susan at the age of two, he was later fostered by a wealthy couple, coolly drowning his adopted brother in the family pool after the lad caught him kissing Susan (Joan Severance) and threatened to snitch to Mom and Pop.

The creepily intense relationship between the two siblings is at the heart of Mel's twisted psyche. His most "normal" treatment of Susan is to use her as bait to gain Vinnie's co-operation and as a reward for his loyalty, something that drives him to tearful, violent rages as he imagines the two of them making love. Only Susan can give her brother his "special treatment": a heroin-amphetamine mix injected between his toes. Relaxed in her arms, Mel flexes his feet and murmurs his catchphrase: "Only the toes knows."

In Spacey's able hands—his own family history tragically tainted by it—the incest theme is never cheapened, made "sexy" or played for laughs. Mel's tirades are both pathetic and frightening. He elicits both our sympathy and our disgust. His death is oddly poetic: when Lococco uses the Malthus bust to smash Mel's amulet, the increasingly paranoid crimelord, his empire crumbling, asks Susan to "send me home."[173] She administers a fatal injection of heroin and builds a Viking funeral pyre, setting Mel's body alight in a rowboat off Long Island Sound. Unable to cope without her beloved brother, Susan goes insane and is committed to a mental hospital, and a disillusioned Terranova quits the Bureau.

Spacey appeared in only seven episodes of *Wiseguy*, but left an indelible impression. As Cannell (who likened life with Mel to being trapped in Hitler's bunker in the closing days of World War II) puts it, "he ripped the cover off the ball every time he was onscreen."[174] Kevin himself has credited the experimental early days of television as the inspiration for his loose-cannon performance, after mentor Lemmon advised him to follow the pioneers of the Fifties and "approach your work with total abandon."[175] "Mel Profitt was the turning point in recognition," Spacey later claimed. "My first lesson in the power of television. I'd walk down the street and people would yell at me, 'Yo, Mel!'"[176]

"I tend to play characters that are on the edge of facing an internal confrontation," Spacey observed in 1989, in one of his first professional interviews: this statement would prove equally valid in 1999. "In many ways, they are characters that are dead, but they don't know it; walking corpses. They're interesting to play because of the complexities.

"I try to give each of these characters a life and a sense of humor; not to just play one dimension of them. That's one of the reasons *Wiseguy* became liked as it did, the character had such a bizarre sense of humor, eccentric. So I tend to be attracted toward roles where there is some crisis. I'm not interested in playing a witty character who stands around with a cocktail glass and makes charming remarks. I definitely like to play people with an edge, and it's probably because I walk on one in my life."[177]

Unable to find another villain as memorable as Mr. Profitt, later seasons of *Wiseguy* resorted to more conventional heavies such as yuppie fashonista Rick Pinzolo and snooty music mogul Winston Newquay–veteran comic Jerry Lewis even put in an appearance. The lack of recognition at awards time must have been galling for Kevin, particularly as Ray Sharkey, playing Mel's predecessor, had received a prestigious Founder's Award from the Viewers for Quality Television committee for his portrayal of Steelgrave. Even the wooden Wahl (who reportedly loathed his scene-stealing co-star)[178] won a Best Actor Golden Globe for the show in 1990.

After *Wiseguy,* Kevin was relegated to background player once more. Hollywood was still stuck in the Brat Pack era, where pretty boys were in vogue: at thirty Spacey looked too old for roles in "college" movies, even while actors his own age like Kevin Bacon and former classmate Val Kilmer continued to play young. "I was offered other series and there were opportunities to, sort of, do more of the same kind of thing," he noted in 1996. "But I just didn't want to become Kevin 'Wiseguy' Spacey for the next five years."[179]

Kevin was paired with Joan Severance again for the limp comedy *See No Evil, Hear No Evil,* a disappointing follow-up to their dynamic alliance on television. *See No Evil* starred Gene Wilder and Richard Pryor, both past their comic prime by several years, in the lead roles of a deaf man and a blind man who inadvertently "witness" a murder. Quite possibly his worst film–though 2005's vapid *Edison* runs it close–and certainly one of his worst performances, Spacey adopts a stiff manner and unconvincingly toffy British accent ("the killahs, Mistah Lyons, the killahs!") to play Kirgo, the pantomime henchman of the piece.

Kevin's increasing frustration with his post-Profitt career is evident in actor Richard E. Grant's filmic memoir *With Nails*. In late 1989, Spacey and Grant worked together on Philip Kaufman's erotic drama *Henry & June*, which chronicles the love triangle between novelist Henry Miller (Fred Ward), his wife June (Uma Thurman), and sultry French writer Anaïs Nin (Maria de Medeiros), in 1930s Paris. It was notable as the first film to receive a NC-17 ("No Children Under 17 Admitted") certificate from the Motion Picture Association of America, which allowed the scenes of lesbian and group sex to pass as "artistic" rather than pornographic–though they appear pretty tame by today's standards.

Spacey, as Miller's libidinous friend Richard Osborn–ironically a thwarted artist himself–despite receiving fifth billing, appears in only a handful of scenes and abruptly disappears two-thirds of the way into the movie. His character's descent into madness happens offscreen and is related in one single exchange between Henry and Anaïs. "Osborn's gone too–gone crazy–really," Ward smirks at one bohemian gathering as Richard's (unnamed) girlfriend weeps in the corner. "They just came and took him away." Spacey was unsatisfied with his marginalised role, as Grant relates in his diary:

> "Kevin is *waiting* to play leads in movies, having done them in the theatre including Broadway. His when-will-it-be-me? *kvech* receives scant support from me."[180]

> "Meet Spacey for a viewing of *Batman* in Les Halles. He is on a rant because he didn't get any close-ups during his scene and has been in heated consultation with his agent and manager...'When

it comes down to it, let's face it, this is just another gig like any other and it's the same old fucking routine and bullshit there always is.'

Kevin is *not* going to stop here, and carries on all the way to *Batman*. On the way back his rage is mercifully waylaid by *Batman's* shortcomings, which he delineates with the precision of a neuro-critic, and which diverts me from my chestful of mucus [Grant was suffering from 'flu during the shoot] and makes me laugh. Which spurs him on to even greater heights. I recognise this syndrome all too acutely and wonder whether having a brontosaurus-sized moan is common to every human or whether it is a particular speciality of actors. Whichever, it's a relief to be merely a spectator at this entertaining outpouring of bile rather than its purveyor."[181]

Perhaps seeking an environment where the lack of close-ups would not trouble him, Spacey returned to the stage to play "Uncle Louie" in the premiere of Neil Simon's *Lost in Yonkers*. In 2000, he described the rather nerve-wracking process of auditioning for the Broadway legend:

"I first met Neil Simon in 1990 in the back rehearsal room of New York's Dramatist Play Services. I was there as one of many actors auditioning for Neil and director Gene Saks for the Broadway production of *Lost in Yonkers*. Nervous and fretful to audition for such a revered playwright, I cracked open the rehearsal room door so I could watch the actor auditioning before me. I saw that Neil was sitting there at a table. He wasn't smiling. I auditioned next and looked up after what I of course thought was a triumphant reading. Neil still wasn't smiling.

Somehow, I was miraculously cast as Uncle Louie and soon began the process of developing the character with Neil, which to this day remains one of my most challenging and joyful professional experiences. We opened in Washington, D.C., on the night that George Bush attacked Kuwait. I will never forget the sight of Neil wringing his hands backstage, muttering to himself that he could already see the headline of the review in tomorrow's paper: "BAGHDAD WASN'T THE ONLY PLACE BOMBS WERE FALLING LAST NIGHT."[182]

After eleven previews, the Broadway production opened on 21st February 1991 at the Richard Rodgers Theatre, where it ran for an impressive 780 performances.[183] Set in 1942, *Yonkers* tells the story of young brothers Jay and Arty, who are left in the care of their intimidating grandmother (Irene Worth) and sweet, childlike aunt Bella (Mercedes Ruehl) in Yonkers, New York, while their debt-addled father Eddie (Mark Blum) works as a travelling scrap iron salesman.

While the relationship between the boys and these two women is the play's primary focus, two other adult children also make an appearance in the narrative. Bella's quasi-mute sister Gert (Lauren Klein) is in two brief scenes while brother Louie, a small-time gangster, features in three substantial ones and adds an element of wry menace with his sub-*Godfather* schtick—"Gee, I hope not. If it went off, I'd have to become a ballerina,"[184] he tells Jay when the boy inquires whether the gun under his belt is loaded. "He's incredible. It's like having a James Cagney movie in your own house,"[185] Arty remarks near the end of Act One.

By Act Two, however, the gloss is off. Angry at his uncle for bullying his younger brother and belittling their hardworking father, Jay challenges him: "What are *you* doing? Hiding in your mother's apartment and scaring little kids and acting like Humphrey Bogart. Well, you're no Humphrey Bogart."[186] Louie is impressed with his nephew's boldness: "You got bigger balls than I thought, Jay. You got a couple of steel basketballs there…"[187] Offstage, Louie ends up enrolling in the Army—more to avoid his fellow hoods than from any patriotic leanings, however.

*Lost in Yonkers* is one of Neil Simon's most celebrated plays, winning the coveted 1991 Pulitzer Prize for Drama. While Spacey's relatively minor role did not command as much attention from critics as the key parts of Grandma Kurnitz and Bella, reviews of his performance were almost universally favourable. *The New York Times* noted that he played Louie with "a commanding mixture of malevolence and avuncularity"[188] —two more common Spacey traits.

"Kevin is a writer's dream," Simon enthused in a 1991 interview. "I could have used him in at least six of my plays, including as Oscar in *The Odd Couple*."[189] Kevin later related how he had added his own flourishes to the character:

> "When Neil left D.C. to gain some distance from the play, I began a ritual of calling him every other day to ask him if it would be okay to make slight adjustments to a scene here, a line there. I did this in such a calculatedly slow and gradual manner that not until the first preview in New York did Neil realize that I had successfully cut 15 lines of his dialogue from ACT I. I cannot begin to describe the torrent of expletives Neil leveled in my direction backstage. I calmly told him I would be happy to discuss the changes, but for the moment I had to go perform ACT II.
>
> We later had a great discussion about the credibility of the character and that my intention was to make him less jokey but not damage his basic persona as a fast-talking, vaudevillian-like gangster. Neil, God bless him, ultimately embraced those changes. On opening night, I received two things from Neil that I will forever cherish: a stunningly beautiful letter from this stunningly gifted playwright and the original, handwritten page of a scene between Uncle Louie and his Ma. It had Moxie written all over it. Oh, I also got one other thing from Neil that night which I will never forget. He was smiling!"[190]

Kevin's embellishments were clearly to the play's advantage: he was subsequently nominated for a Tony Award for the role as Best Featured Actor. *Lost in Yonkers* also received Tony nominations for Best Play, Best Leading Actress (Ruehl), Best Featured Actress (Worth) and Best Director (Gene Saks). Only Saks went home from the ceremony at New York's Minskoff Theater empty-handed: on 2nd June 1991, after a full ten years of treading the boards, Kevin Spacey was finally accorded the recognition from the theatrical community he deserved.

Addressing Simon in his acceptance speech, Spacey said: "Neil, the last award that I ever got, I was 18 years old and I was at Chatsworth High

School in Southern California and I did a monologue from [Simon's 1970 play] *The Gingerbread Lady* at the fall drama festival and I won best actor, so thanks again." Ironically, the only major male character in this play (which was the basis for the 1981 film *Only When I Laugh*) is a middle-aged gay actor still stuck in off-Broadway bit parts after 22 years in the business: his bitter tirades ("What kills me is that I'm so good. I'm such a good actor I can't stand it...I was born too talented and too late...Oh God, I want to be a star so bad")[191] are not unlike the discontented Spacey's comments to Richard E. Grant on the *Henry & June* set.

Not that the accolade impressed the movie world much. While the Tonys are often described as "the Oscars of live theatre," in reality they count for very little in Hollywood, something that was made sharply clear to Spacey when *Yonkers* was adapted into a feature film two years later. Worth and Ruehl made the cut, but Kevin's role was given to Academy Award-winning actor Richard Dreyfuss.[192]

Although Kevin Spacey played leading roles in two well-regarded TV movie biopics in the early 1990s, as disgraced televangelist Jim Bakker in *Fall From Grace* (1990) and crusading lawyer Clarence Darrow in *Darrow* (1991), major parts in cinematic releases proved harder to come by. He was cast in *Glengarry Glen Ross* after Al Pacino, impressed with *Lost in Yonkers*, recommended him to director James Foley. "It was depressing to be shooting a movie in which the greatest actors around were calling me a pussy every day for six, seven weeks. I felt like I was the pillar in the center of a storm, being assaulted from all sides," Spacey later noted.

"One day, Pacino chewed me a new asshole. Al, unbeknownst to me, had asked the sound guys not to do sound. The camera was on me and Al started improvising: 'Kevin, you fucking piece of shit!' I thought, Did he just say Kevin? He didn't let up; it got very personal. I looked like a car wreck. But at the end of the scenes, he walked over and put his arm around me and said, 'That was terrific.'"[193]

In 1992, shortly after making a notable guest appearance as an eccentric tycoon in the TV drama series *L.A. Law*, Kevin scored his first co-starring cinematic role in Alan J. Pakula's risible domestic thriller

*Consenting Adults.* The first Spacey movie to examine the dark underbelly of suburbia (as he would do rather more successfully in *American Beauty* some seven years later), *Consenting Adults* concerns two couples, Richard and Priscilla Parker (Kevin Kline and Mary Elizabeth Mastrantonio), and their new neighbours Eddy and Kay Otis (Spacey and Rebecca Miller).

As had been the case with *Les Liaisons Dangereuses,* the director had to fight the project's producers to get the still-somewhat-obscure "guy with the receding hair from New York" cast. This is how Spacey was described by one executive to Curtis Hanson, who was unable to offer him the leading male role in the film *The Hand That Rocks The Cradle*, released the same year as *Consenting Adults*, after the same studio (Hollywood Pictures, a Disney subsidiary) insisted on a bigger name. "I had tried to cast Kevin several times over the years, and never been allowed to. He was not acceptable to the studio, they thought he was too offbeat,"[194] Hanson revealed in 2002.

"I suppose [Hollywood Pictures] thought I would have been nice as the driver or the boat captain, but not in this leading role opposite Kevin Kline," Spacey told *Premiere* in a contemporary interview. "So Alan, bless him, fought for me in a way that you always dream someone will—especially in Hollywood, where chances are often tough for actors who don't look a certain way...

"I've played supporting roles in films for a while, in the hope that I would learn something...But it's a frustrating experience, because the relationship that you're searching for with a director doesn't really occur. Directors feel that if they've hired a competent actor in that small role, then they can concentrate on the three or four actors who move the plot along."[195] Kevin certainly took the part seriously, bleaching his hair and losing almost 30 pounds through a vigorous physical training programme to play the superfit Eddy.[196]

The nominal "hero" of *Consenting Adults*, Richard Parker, is an embryonic Lester Burnham. Stuck in a job he hates (composing advertising jingles), he is chastised by his wife for his staid attitude to life–"[Eddy] may not always play by the rules but at least he's in the game," she tells him after their ebullient new friend fakes a car accident to get the Parkers out of debt. Attracted to the voluptuous Kay, Richard is persuaded by Eddy to forsake his "50 percent existence," at least for an evening. "I wonder what would happen if you and I got up in the middle of the night, went next door and crept into the other man's bedroom…" whispers Kevin II enticingly.

In best Spacey style, it's all a scam. Richard duly arrives at Eddy's house, sleeps with a woman who appears to be Kay, and then returns home, only for "Kay" to be found bludgeoned to death by a baseball bat the next morning. Clever Eddy didn't spend the night with Mrs. P. at all and has a cast-iron alibi, while Richard, having inadvertently implicated himself, is charged with the crime. Priscilla divorces her husband and takes up with Eddy, however, when he recognises her voice on a radio talent show, an out-on-bail Richard realises that Kay is alive (quite how he didn't notice that the woman he made love to was not his comely neighbour in the first place is never explained).

Having discovered that Eddy is attempting to collect a $1.5 million indemnity claim on his wife, Richard tracks Kay to a seedy motel and confronts her. Shortly thereafter Eddy, who has been tracking the pair, gives Kay the "bat treatment" and slips away. Now implicated in a second murder, Richard flees.

Fortunately for him, Priscilla discovers the plane ticket Eddy used on the night of the fake Kay's death and realises the truth. Richard performs a commando-style raid on Eddy's home and Eddy, now in full-on crazed mode, reveals to Priscilla his plans to dispatch the pair of (nosey) Parkers. After the obligatory physical smasheroo between the two Kevins, the good wife steps in and coshes Eddy with–yup–another baseball bat just as he is about to gun Richard down. The final scene shows a reconciled Richard and Priscilla moving into a very secluded house–with no neighbours visible for miles.

Ineptly plotted and ploddingly-directed, with a dreary lead performance from Kline and a histrionic one from Mastrantonio, *Consenting Adults* nevertheless boasts a fine showing from Spacey, his creepily charismatic hustler the movie's only saving grace. During his final confrontation with the other Kevin, you almost want the devious conman to win–in the film's most striking shot, the camera lingers on Eddy's splayed body as Richard and Priscilla leave the room. Fixated on the real draw, we barely notice them go.

As one contemporary reviewer noted: "No one makes for a better nut case than Kevin Spacey. In both television and movie roles, he has flitted around the edges of stardom for years, doing marvelously peculiar turns that more often than not steal the thunder of the bigger-name performers. And, as Eddy, he is given his first real opportunity to fully express his fruitcake talent...In the end, it's the lusty, Mad Hatter gleam in Spacey's eyes that sticks with us. Even when the movie asks us to suspend our disbelief far beyond what is reasonable, he deliciously spins his web. In a just universe, his name should become a household word."[197] Just three years later, it would be.

# Chapter Six

# Spacey and Fowler

*"My dad and I...There were things we hadn't discussed until the last year of his life, and we had a grand number of conversations in which we...He understood my point of view, and I understood his point of view and forgave him. I realised I couldn't have done any better in his shoes, given his circumstances."*
–Kevin Spacey (2008)[198]

*"If you presume something about another person, it leads you to make all kinds of assumptions. If your perception is wrong, it can lead to tragedy..."*
–Kevin Spacey on *American Beauty* (1999)[199]

On New Year's Day, 1990, Kevin's brother Randy received a phone call from Kathleen Fowler informing him that Geoff was "a little under the weather." When pressed, she told her son that his father was dehydrated and urinating blood–clearly more than "a little under the weather." Randy suggested that Kathleen take Geoff to hospital; Kathleen, who had gone along with her husband–as always–when he became a Christian Scientist in the early 1960s, refused to do so. In line with their faith, she said, she would "heal" him through prayer.

The temptation to leave the life of the man who had made his childhood such a misery to fate must have been a strong one, however Randy overruled his mother and called 911, arranging for an ambulance to collect his father (at the time, both the Fowler parents and their elder son were living in Washington State). Julie and Kevin flew in from their respective homes–the younger brother toting a giant stuffed gorilla toy for Geoff and a miniature tape machine to secretly record any conversations with the medical staff–and the reassembled clan gathered in Randy's apartment to wait for news. Geoff duly recovered and was discharged from hospital a couple of weeks later; the family dispersed. They would never come together as a complete unit again.[200]

Geoff and Kathleen Fowler, in what would prove to be their final move as a couple, relocated to Lawrenceville, Georgia, in November 1991, using some of the funds from Kathleen's 1985 lottery win to purchase a large brick-fronted property with five bedrooms plus a gourmet kitchen, games room, exercise room and sun deck. Increasingly frail in his later years, Geoff Fowler died during an emergency operation in the late evening on 24th December 1992.

His younger son's minor celebrity earned Geoff an obituary notice in trade bible *Variety*, which described the deceased as "a writer and business consultant and father of actor Kevin Spacey."[201] An additional obituary in *The Atlanta Constitution* reflected his sporadic employment history, noting: "He was a reporter and editor with various newspapers from 1951 to 1963, and later worked for the Rockwell Corp., Xerox Corp., Litton and the Bechtel Corp." Worryingly, given Geoff's history of abuse towards his elder son, the article also revealed that "Mr Fowler was a Scoutmaster and served in various offices with the Boy Scouts of America in Wyoming, Colorado and California."[202]

In 1999, Kevin said that it was "typical" of Geoff to pass at such a time—"My mother and I figure he did it on purpose. You're celebrating Christmas, the most beautiful time of the year to come together with your family, and then you're like, 'Oh right, it's also the anniversary of...' Fucker! You know he did that on purpose."[203]

While he has always maintained that his mother was a devoted supporter of his chosen profession—"[she] used to leave work early, drive me to acting class, go for a coffee somewhere, come back and pick me up, take me on to another class...I owe her a lot"[204]—Spacey has been less forthcoming about his father's attitude. He once related that it was not until Geoff saw his performance in *Lost in Yonkers* that he "believed [I'd] make a living."[205] The date is telling: by 1988, three years before *Yonkers*, Spacey had already played credited parts in three theatrical movies and several Broadway shows, as well as garnering critical acclaim and a steadily-growing fanbase for his portrayal of Mel Profitt. If that wasn't "making a living," what was?

"My father used to have all these conversations with me about being an actor," Spacey told *The Guardian's* William Leith in 2002, "and how difficult that was going to be. And he was most worried that I was going to go through a life that was similar to his, of being unemployed. For a long time he wasn't sure that it was going to work out for me. What drove me was a determination to not have the frustration in life that my father experienced, and also to make him quite proud, to make him relax, and to make him realise that it was okay, that everything was going to be fine."[206]

In recent years–perhaps as a reaction to Randy's revelations in *The Mail on Sunday*–Spacey has been more sympathetic towards his father's employment situation and claimed that Geoff always encouraged his decision to take up dramatics:

> "The idea of being an actor occurred to me at a young age–and my mother and father both gave me absolute support from the get-go. They never said, 'You've got to have something to fall back on.' Instead, they said, 'Great. What can we do to help?' By high school, I had become obsessed with drama. I'm the guy who did all the plays. I was directing plays, I was doing one-acts, I was doing festivals, doing musicals, I worked in summer theater. There always seemed to be 13 plates spinning."[207]

Kevin seems to have forgiven his father for constantly uprooting the family and the subsequent trauma he endured as a result, albeit not until Geoff–an erudite man, despite his unsuccessful career–was close to death and no longer capable of speech himself. As he related to *Maxim* in 2001: "The last series of conversations that we had [was] when he was in the intensive care unit and they had cut his throat for a tracheotomy, so he couldn't speak. He had to listen. There were a lot of things that I said [over] the course of that couple of weeks that I don't think I could've ever said in any other circumstance. But by the end, we'd said a lot of things to each other. I think by the end there was an understanding and a reconciliation that we'd never experienced before."[208]

Spacey has credited Geoff–who gave his children penmanship lessons on Sunday afternoons–with passing on his appreciation of the literary arts. "We had reading night," he said in 2001. "We used to read from great novels, so I was introduced at a very young age to Faulkner and Hemingway. It's held me in very good stead for being able to judge material."[209]

"In a weird way, I'm grateful for what happened to me as a child," Kevin said in 2003. "It was what it is like being an actor. You're uprooted constantly, put in new situations, plucked out of one thing and thrown into another. Every three months you have a new family. It allowed me to make those emotional adjustments and realise that life was just going to be this continual kind of re-inventing and shifting."[210] In 2006, he added: "It was tough, but I adapted to it and turned it into a virtue. I have photos of people who've meant something to me. It brings me comfort to look across the room and see someone's cheeky smile."[211]

This periodic early relocation has left Spacey with a compulsion to re-arrange things, as he noted in a 1999 interview:

> "I move furniture around. This is how bad it is: My friends'll come around for dinner and then they'll come back again a few weeks later to play with the dogs or bring their kids to hang out, and the furniture will probably have changed four or five times since then. They'll go, 'Hey, Kevin, wasn't the couch over there before?' 'Yeah.' 'So why did you move it?' And I can't tell them why. 'I don't know. I guess I just didn't like it over there anymore.' I can't stop moving furniture, and I do it alone at 3 in the morning…I have a whole process."[212]

After Geoff's passing, Kevin was finally able to enter the office where he kept his papers. "The bookcases in his office were lined, lined, lined with notebooks that he had written," Spacey recalled in 2003. "Stories. And then on one bookshelf was his novel that he'd been writing since 1963…It was like discovering somebody who obviously had this whole other life. It was so weird to suddenly be awakened to this passion that he had."[213]

"It's like my father created his own alternate universe," Kevin said in 1996. "He had all this stuff in his brain–this amazing sense of humor, this love for the twenties and thirties, this awesome style. But no one ever knew…"[214] In her 1984 letter to her offspring, Kathleen defended her husband's lack of productivity, claiming that their home "was never conducive to quiet, contemplative work." She added: "Randall was in the garage with several other teenagers playing the drums; Kevin was in the house singing and tap dancing and the telephone rang all the time...No one ever considered Dad or what he was trying to do–his writing efforts always came last after everything else. Everyone wanted to do "their own thing" and DID–that is, everyone but Dad."[215]

Spacey has spoken in the past of trying to get Geoff's novel published[216]– however, to date this has not happened and the true content of the book remains unknown, even to Kevin's two siblings. The less benign of Geoff's articles, the anti-Semitic and pornographic tracts, were presumably swiftly disposed of. As Randy notes: "Nobody really knows what [Geoff] was doing all the time he was shut up alone in his office. Except Kevin: my brother grabbed all my father's papers after the old man died and he's never offered to show my sister or me what's in them."[217]

In the same 2002 *Guardian* interview cited above, Spacey revealed that discovering the existence of his father's secret tome had affected him greatly:

> "What was the book about? Spacey shakes his head. For a moment, he seems slightly choked. He writes himself, he tells me, but he won't give specifics. 'I write all the time,' he says. 'I write all the time. Because I think I have to. I have to find out whether I can do it or not. It has to do with my father. More than anything else, it has to do with him.'"[218]

A year later, Kevin appeared in the film *The United States of Leland* as the father of a teenager who kills his girlfriend's autistic brother in a misguided attempt to release him from "all the sadness" of the outside world. Spacey's character, the "despicable" (in the eyes of one social worker) Albert T. Fitzgerald, is acerbic, coldly humorous, remote–and a famous author, the intense, moving prose from which he has gained his celebrity status his only outlet for expressing any love for the son he hardly sees.

"He's a bastard, so what? You don't judge a writer by his life," the boy's teacher (Don Cheadle), an aspiring novelist himself, remarks early on in the film, "you judge him by his work. It's a different moral standard going on here." "I'm not really–that adept at gauging people's emotional reactions to events," Spacey tells him, when questioned about Leland's state of mind at the time of the murder. "I disagree, I've read your books," Cheadle counters. "So have I," says Kevin. "They haven't helped."

As well as playing Fitzgerald, Kevin also produced the film via Trigger Street–writer/director Matthew Ryan Hoge, who used his own experiences teaching at a juvenile hall in Los Angeles as the basis of the film, was another Spacey protégé. "I think a lot of the reason [Spacey took the role], to be candid, was because he wanted to get the movie made…He knew I wanted him to play the part. I kept asking him and bugging him,"[219] Hoge later said. Kevin played another writer in a 1985 theatrical production of Anton Chekhov's *The Seagull* (retitled *A Seagull*), the temperamental Konstantin, who realises too late that "whatever one has to say should come straight from the heart"[220] and is eventually driven to suicide by the poor reception his work receives.

In a 2005 interview with *Premiere*, Spacey stated: "I admire the craft of writing more than anything."[221] "I suppose I have some bizarre idea that it would be great to be a writer," he noted in 2007, when asked what career path he would have chosen if he had not discovered acting. "I find it an astounding gift to be able to have nothing come between your heart and the page…"[222]

Between his father's "heart and the page," it seems, there was plenty: the secret novel was not the only surprising thing that Kevin came across among Geoff's effects. As he related to *Esquire's* Amy Raphael shortly after his interview with William Leith, "what was most startling was finding letters he'd written to me when I was a student at Juilliard–long, handwritten letters which he had never sent. Warning of the evils of the world…I read them and thought, 'Why couldn't you have sent them? Letters are meant to be shared!'"[223]

It is difficult to establish exactly what effect Geoff's warped worldview had on his daily family life. Registered as a Republican affiliate in 1950, it is known that he was also an active and enthusiastic member of the American Nazi Party, keeping a picture of Adolf Hitler on the mantelpiece at his various abodes and even styling his moustache and hair to resemble the Fascist leader's for a period in the 1960s. As Randy related to *The Mail on Sunday's* Sharon Churcher in 2004:

> "Kevin, Julie and I weren't allowed to have any friends at the house. I think my father was afraid they'd discover what he was keeping in his office…I was allowed to join the Scouts but after my 12th birthday, Dad made me quit because the new scoutmaster was Jewish, and Kevin was never even allowed to be a Cub Scout. By then Dad had joined the Nazi Party and we'd have to sit in silence at dinner while he lectured us on how white Anglo-Saxons were better than anyone else and the Holocaust was a lie and the Jews ran Hollywood and the banks."[224]

The full extent to which Geoff tried to impose his bigoted views on his younger son, however, is unclear. "[Geoff] never foisted any information onto any of you," Kathleen asserted in her 1984 letter, with reference to "Dad's "political" interests," "he is not trying to make you accept his opinions, his philosophy, his understanding of history, what he actually saw and heard while overseas. All of this information or any part of it was given to you because you asked. You can accept it, refute it, or do your own research and come up with your own opinions."[225]

Kevin's own political allegiances emerged early. A staunch Democrat, he canvassed for Jimmy Carter while still in high school and later worked the campaign trail for Ted Kennedy and Bill Clinton, becoming a close ally of Clinton's–by Spacey's 2002 reckoning "the most progressive, the most effective, the most hardworking, the most dedicated president we've ever had"[226]–after their initial meeting at a fundraising event in 1992 (Bill once made a phone call to Kathleen from Air Force One: she thought it was Kevin playing a prank).

To commemorate the final weeks of his presidency, the outgoing Clinton made a tongue-in-cheek, home video-style film in which he gives a mock acceptance speech in front of a mirror whilst brandishing an Oscar–"Ever since I was a little boy I've wanted to be a real–actor!"–only for Spacey to nonchalantly sidle up to him and take his statuette back. Bill even claimed at one Democratic gathering that "Getting to be friends with Kevin has been one of the best perks of being president."[227]

As one London socialite noted after meeting both men: "They are very much alike. For the half hour or however long you are in their company, the spotlight shines on you alone."[228] Despite his long history of campaigning, Kevin has shown little inclination towards running for government himself, once declaring that he would "rather become a crack addict"[229] than a politician.

Spacey accompanied his chum Clinton to a British Labour Party rally in Blackpool in October 2002 (alongside another Premier pal, then-Prime Minister Tony Blair),[230] and entertained the delegates with his perfect impersonation of Clinton's Arkansas drawl, later sharing a meal in a local McDonalds with the former President and Blair's P.R. guru Alistair Campbell. Spacey and Clinton, together with black comic Chris Tucker, travelled to Africa in September of the same year, pledging money from the newly-formed Clinton Foundation to raise awareness about the AIDS epidemic and to try to combat its lethal spread across the continent—what Geoff would have made of this trip is not hard to imagine.

It also seems unlikely that Fowler senior—who applauded the assassinations of civil rights leader Martin Luther King and the anti-apartheid elder Kennedy siblings[231]—would have approved of some of his son's role choices. Journalist Wes Brent in *The Murder of Mary Phagan*, for example, an initially unprincipled character who is eventually persuaded to reject the anti-Semitic prejudices of his meal ticket, solicitor general Hugh Dorsey. Or liberal attorney Clarence Darrow (one of Spacey's favourite parts), who in defending a young black man who shot two white thugs in self-defence makes an impassioned plea to the jury for racial tolerance.

"Suppose you were a Negro," says Kevin-as-Darrow, "suppose every day of your life you sat down to supper with your parents and your grandparents and you saw in their eyes and on their bodies the scars of bondage and hatred visited upon them by white men! The law has made the Negro equal, but Man has not…"[232] In 1996, three-and-a-half years after Geoff's passing, Spacey appeared in the film *A Time To Kill* as Darrow's polar opposite, smug D.A. Rufus Buckley—"He's mean, he's ambitious and he's gonna eat this up because of the publicity"—who presses for the death penalty for a black man charged with murdering the two white supremacists who violated his young daughter.

In recent years, Spacey has played several characters with abusive fathers. Teacher Eugene Simonet's emotional scars in *Pay It Forward* (2000) are reflected in his physical ones. As a boy, the alcoholic Simonet senior coshed him with a wooden plank and doused him with petrol before setting him alight as "punishment" for running away from home. "The last thing I remember…I'll never forget it–were his eyes, his eyes, because they were filled with this–immense satisfaction,"[233] a tearful Spacey-as-Eugene relates. Ultra-passive Quoyle (we never learn his first name)[234] in *The Shipping News* (2001) is a punchbag first for his father and then his slatternly New York wife, before at last finding peace with a local woman in the sleepy Newfoundland town of his ancestors.

*The Shipping News's* opening scene shows Guy Quoyle (John Dunsworth) standing on a pier, trying to teach his son to swim by taunting the boy as he struggles in the water. "I used to imagine that I'd been given to the wrong family at birth and that somewhere in the world my real people longed for me," says a doleful Kevin in voiceover. "From where my father stood my failure to dog-paddle was only the first of many failures…I stumbled into adulthood learning to separate my feelings from my life."

Quoyle senior's list includes "failure to make friends every time we moved to another dreary upstate town"–not so far from the young Kevin's own experiences in 1960s California, perhaps. "[Quoyle] has no sense of himself. He's just been squashed down, abused emotionally, possibly battered by his father…"[235] Spacey mused in 2002.

Later in the film, Guy's darkest secret is revealed. As a teenager, he raped and impregnated his twelve-year-old half-sister. "When someone hurts you that much, how do you–does it ever go away, is it possible?" Quoyle asks his aunt (played as an adult by Judi Dench)–poignantly, this is one of the few moments where Spacey seems credible in the role, a part he lobbied for after reading the source novel six years earlier and "falling in love"[236] with it. "When I read the book, I identified with the man,"[237] he claimed in one 2001 interview.

The Spacey movie character that most evokes Geoff Fowler, however, was not played by Kevin himself. The actor recalled "nearly falling out of bed"[238] when he first read the screenplay for the film that would win him his second Oscar, *American Beauty* (1999)–perhaps his father was on his mind. The neighbour of Spacey's Lester Burnham, Colonel Frank Fitts (played by Chris Cooper, who also appeared with Kevin in *Darrow* and *A Time To Kill*), a Nazi memorabilia collector, brutal child beater and repressed homosexual, is eerily similar to the Geoff that Randy describes.

There are also less malign parallels between the two men. Spacey has often criticised Fowler senior's apparent obsession with material possessions:

> "I think he always fancied himself as an aristocrat. He admired things of that kind of sophistication; leather-bound books, beautiful watches, cufflinks...There was a time when my parents actually had plastic on the fucking *furniture*. Have you ever seen that before? I would have huge arguments with my dad, asking him why. He'd say it was to keep the sofa clean, but I'd always want to know why he couldn't clean it after someone has sat on it. I was like, 'How can we ask anyone over and ask them to sit on *plastic*?' So I began to rebel against all that very early on. Oh yeah. Oh yeah."[239]

Such censure of consumerist culture is one of the main themes of *American Beauty*, as is illustrated in the extract below. Like *Sunset Boulevard's* Joe Gillis, Lester's story is told from beyond the grave. Spacey's opening voiceover informs us that "My name is Lester Burnham. This is my neighbourhood. This is my street. This...is my life. I'm forty-two years old. In less than a year, I'll be dead."

We first see Lester as his "American Dream" lifestyle is souring. Stuck in a dreary office job, he is despised by his wife, ambitious real-estate broker Carolyn (Annette Bening) and barely registers with his sullen teenage daughter Jane (Thora Birch). Frequent Spacey collaborator Peter Gallagher features in the film as realtor Buddy Kane, with whom Carolyn has an affair. "In a way, I'm dead already," Kevin deadpans.

After watching a high school basketball game at which Jane is a cheerleader, Lester develops an infatuation with her seemingly-sexually precocious friend Angela (played by Mena Suvari, who bears a striking resemblance to Joan Severance, the actress who portrayed Mel Profitt's sister-lover Susan). When he overhears Angela say that she would sleep with him if he had more muscle, Lester completely changes his lifestyle. Blackmailing his boss into firing him, he takes up low-pressure employment at a fast-food outlet, smokes marijuana bought from Fitts's son Ricky (Wes Bentley), and starts running and lifting weights in the garage so that he can "look good naked."

The character of Lester has often been compared to Jack Lemmon's initially-meek office clerk C.C. Baxter in *The Apartment*, released the year after Spacey was born. Trapped in a dull desk job with few prospects, Baxter allows his philandering superiors to use his own home as a love nest in order to gain a promotion. "I used to live like Robinson Crusoe—I mean shipwrecked, among eight million people, and then one day I saw a footprint in the sand—and there you were," Baxter says after experiencing his own Angela-esque moment with überboss J.D.'s mistress Fran Kubelik (played by Shirley MacLaine, the sister-in-law of Spacey's *Beauty* co-star Annette Bening), who takes an overdose of sleeping pills in Baxter's apartment when her relationship with J.D. falls apart.

Director Sam Mendes noted: "While we were shooting *American Beauty* [Kevin and I] talked a lot about *The Apartment* and the way Lemmon made that character so real and normal, right down to the way his hair changed through the course of the movie, becoming both more and more distressed and yet more and more true to his inner self."[240] Discovering a new enjoyment of life, Lester sees his wife's empty preoccupation with "stuff" for what it is:

LESTER

Christ, Carolyn. When did you become so... joyless?

CAROLYN

*(taken aback)*

Joyless?! I am not joyless! There happens to be a lot about me that you don't know, mister smarty man. There is plenty of joy in my life.

LESTER
*(leaning toward her)*
Whatever happened to that girl who used to fake seizures at frat parties when she got bored? And who used to run up to the roof of our first apartment building to flash the traffic helicopters? Have you totally forgotten about her? Because I haven't.

*His face is close to hers, and suddenly the atmosphere is charged. She pulls back automatically, but it's clear she's drawn to him. He smiles, and moves even closer, holding his beer loosely balanced. Then, just before their lips meet...*

CAROLYN
*(barely audible)*
Lester. You're going to spill beer on the couch.

*She's immediately sorry she said it, but it's too late. His smile fades, and the moment is gone.*

LESTER
So what? It's just a couch.

CAROLYN
This is a four thousand-dollar sofa upholstered in Italian silk. This is not "just a couch."

LESTER
It's just a couch!

*He stands and gestures toward all the things in the room.*

LESTER (cont'd)
This isn't life. This is just stuff. And it's become more important to you than living. Well, honey, that's just nuts.

*Carolyn stares at him, on the verge of tears, then turns and*
*walks out of the room before he can see her cry.*

LESTER (cont'd)
*(calls after her)*
I'm only trying to help you.[241]

The family next door are even more dysfunctional than the Burnhams. The fascistic Colonel Fitts has cowed wife Barbara (Alison Janney) into a state of near-catatonia and abandoned his son in a mental hospital for two years (intriguingly Ricky, like the mythically-rebellious young Kevin, was sent to military school to teach him "discipline" and expelled for fighting).

Fitts reacts with disgust upon meeting the only pair in the film who seem truly content with their domestic arrangements, a gay couple–"How come these faggots always have to rub it in your face?" and, after watching Ricky and Lester's drug rendezvous through the garage window, mistakenly concludes that the two are engaged in a sexual relationship. Ricky, seeing a chance to escape his repressive household, tells his father he "sucks dick for money" and goads Fitts into throwing him out.

At the film's close, sexual secrets are revealed. The slutty Angela is actually a virgin and avowed homophobe Frank, who approaches Lester in the garage and startles him with a kiss, is (surprise, surprise) a closeted gay man. Screenwriter Alan Ball, who is openly gay, modelled Fitts on his own homosexually-repressed father, also named Frank. "My father was never violent, but he was deeply conflicted in certain ways that are similar to the Colonel,"[242] Ball said in 2000.

Rebuffed by his neighbour, Frank flees home in shame. Lester finds a distressed Angela in his lounge and she tells him she thinks he's sexy. On learning of her virginity, however, he is unable to seduce her and instead comforts the crying girl with a paternal hug (his name is an anagram of "Humbert Learns," a nod to the protagonist of Vladimir Nabokov's controversial 1955 novel *Lolita*, Humbert Humbert). Unlike him, Lester ultimately rejects the opportunity to seduce his young object of desire.

After Angela leaves the room, Lester picks up an old picture of himself and Carolyn with a younger Jane. As he smiles at the snap a gunshot rings out: the rejected Frank has taken his revenge. Despite his death, Lester is content, explaining in the final voiceover that it is "hard to stay mad, when there's so much beauty in the world." As Lester discovers over the course of the movie, true "beauty" comes from his rediscovered love of life, work and family, not the sterile, inanimate "stuff" around him. He learns a lesson that Fitts does not.

Colonel Fitts has plastic on his couch. Just like Geoff Fowler.

*Young Kathleen Knutson with her parents Harriet and Allen in 1935.*

*Kathleen with her half-sister Jane in 1943.*

*Thomas Geoffrey Fowler with his half-siblings Nancy, Stephen and Susan in 1940.*

*Geoff in Europe during his war service, mid 1940s.*

*Kathleen and Geoff on their wedding day, 14 February 1949.*

*A very young Kevin with his mother.*

*Kevin as a toddler with his father.*

*Brothers Kevin and Randy at home in 1963.*

*Kevin and Randy in Lodi, California, in 1969.*

*Kevin strikes a pose for his brother in 1971, staging a bicycle crash.*

*Kevin and Randy in February 1972, shortly before leaving Northridge Military Academy.*

*Kevin performing at the Busch Gardens park in Van Nuys, California, in 1978.*

*Kevin entertaining his family with his Johnny Carson impressions
at his parents' home in Los Angeles, January 1979.*

*Kevin playing Randy's drums, Christmas 1979.*

*Kevin with his parents during the* Ghosts *run in 1982.*

*Kevin and Randy at Randy's home in Washington State in 1990.*

*Kevin with Aunt Jane, Kathleen, and Legacy outside the Fowler home in Lawrenceville, Georgia, January 1993.*

*Kevin and Randy in Los Angeles, February 2003.*

*Kevin signing autographs outside the Old Vic following a performance of* The Philadelphia Story *in 2005.*

# Chapter Seven

# Keyser Spacey

*"Nobody knows who I am yet. And I want to keep it that way. The longer I do, the better off I'll be as an actor. Success is like death. The more successful you become, the higher the houses in the hills get and the higher the fences get."*
—Kevin Spacey (1991)[243]

*"And like that—poof! He's gone."*
—Verbal Kint on Keyser Söze, *The Usual Suspects* (1995)

After his quirky turn in *Consenting Adults*, Kevin Spacey spent the rest of the early Nineties alternating between supporting roles in theatrical films, TV movies and the odd guest spot on a TV show. He also made several audio book recordings that were released on cassette during this time: *Exceptional Clearance* by William J. Caunitz (1991), *Mrs. God* by Peter Straub (1991), *Night Squad* by David Goodis (1992), *The Agenda: Inside the Clinton White House* by Bob Woodward (1994) and *Nobody's Fool* by Richard Russo (1994).[244]

Kevin played a cynical, typically "Spaceyesque" news hack in the Disney film *Iron Will* (1994) and another suburban husband, Lloyd Chasseur, in the underrated black comedy *The Ref* (also 1994),[245] partnered with the fiery Australian actress Judy Davis as a warring couple held hostage on Christmas Eve by a gunman (Denis Leary). Spacey gets in some good training for his spats with Annette Bening in *American Beauty*—"The day you see anything through to the end, I'll stick my own dick in my ear!"—before Leary's increasingly aggressive presence forces the pair to reconcile their differences.

The opening scene of the movie, in which the bilious Chasseurs visit a tetchy marriage guidance counsellor, could have come straight out of *Beauty*. "We haven't had sex in quite a while…by our twelfth anniversary, we had gotten into a pretty stale routine…it's no wonder I had an affair," sighs Davis, as Spacey sneers: "How could you tell him all that so casually like you were asking for a glass of water…why don't you have oral sex too, I'll go wait in the car?" Davis's character is named "Caroline," almost identical to Bening's "Carolyn."

"You think my life turned out the way I want it because I live in this house?" Kevin demands of his captor, in another pre-Lester nod. "You think every time I look in the mirror I shout 'Gee, I'm glad I'm me and not some nineteen-year-old billionaire rock star with the body of an athlete and a 24 hour erection?'" "Spacey is hilarious," noted Jami Bernard in *The New York Daily News*, "a fine stage actor who has been shamefully underused in movies."[246]

Spacey would soon be "underused" no more. His next film, *Swimming With Sharks*, on which he also served as co-producer, marked the beginning of an incredibly successful period for the actor comparable with Robert De Niro's domination of the screen in the late 1970s and Marlon Brando's in the early 1950s.

Shot on a tiny budget in just eighteen days, *Sharks* was scripted and directed by George Huang and is allegedly based on his own experiences on the lowest rung of the Hollywood ladder at Universal and Columbia Pictures. Spacey plays caustic exec Buddy Ackerman, who torments his long-suffering assistant Guy (Frank Whaley) by constantly berating him–"If you were in my toilet bowl I wouldn't bother flushing it! My bathmat means more to me than you!"–forcing him to run menial errands, and stealing his script ideas.

After discovering that his producer girlfriend Dawn (Michelle Forbes) has also been sleeping with Buddy, Guy eventually snaps, taking his boss hostage in his apartment at gunpoint (the story is told in a series of flashbacks). Guy employs a rather novel form of torture, punching Buddy in the face and splashing hot sauce and lemon juice into the wounds, and then slicing his tongue with an envelope–"Paper cuts, now they can be a bitch!" When Buddy tearfully relates the story of his wife's murder in a carjacking incident, Guy appears to relent, despite Buddy's masochistic encouragement after Dawn arrives on the scene—"C'mon, let's finish this. Give it to me! Show me what you're made of!"—but then raises his gun…

*Swimming With Sharks* has its faults. The climax, in which a now-corrupted Guy elects to shoot Dawn instead of Buddy, seems contrived and artificial, and Whaley makes rather a dull hero. However, the film has a great asset in its other central figure. As was the case with *Consenting Adults*, Spacey steals every scene in which he appears with his deliciously vicious tirades. "When Spacey goes ballistic," Owen Gleiberman stated in *Entertainment Weekly*, "only to freeze the nitroglycerine in his veins a moment later, you don't want to look anywhere else."[247]

Kevin is years too young for the part—Buddy is supposed to be a generation clear of Guy, who is a rather mature looking 25—but few viewers minded. As *The New York Times's* Janet Maslin observed: "Mr. Spacey's Buddy is a caricature so dazzling that even Buddy might have to say something nice about it: cool, withering, studiously suave, and spurred by impulses that might seem peevish even in a 2-year-old child."[248] Villainous credentials now firmly established, Kevin's electrifying showing in *Sharks* was followed by a shocking turn as a killer who takes his pound of flesh—literally—in *Se7en*.

In between these two movies, there was the one that would net Kevin Spacey his first Academy Award. Check a list of the best films ever made—any list—and odds are *The Usual Suspects* will be on there. *Se7en, L.A. Confidential* and *American Beauty,* three other Spacey-starrers, may also make the cut, but *Suspects* is a dead cert. As the faux-cripple criminal mastermind Roger "Verbal" Kint, a.k.a. Keyser Söze, Spacey shone out even amongst an ensemble cast who were also giving career-best performances, including another future Oscar winner, Benicio Del Toro.

The street-smart, sardonic, slightly sinister fellow who is never quite what he appears to be—now considered the "classic" Spacey characterisation—surely finds its finest example in Söze. Kevin's chameleon-like ability to transform his appearance between roles is remarkable. The hollow-cheeked, fragile Verbal, with his bent frame and hair shaped into a widow's peak (the actor filed down his shoes and glued his fingers together to make his shambling movements more authentic), is a world away from both the tanned, healthy Angeleno of *Swimming With Sharks* and the bald, bulky intellectual of *Se7en*.

Spacey's casting in *The Usual Suspects* seemed perfect, and for good reason. Two years previously, he had attended a screening of director Bryan Singer's first film, *Public Access*, at the Sundance Film Festival, and was so impressed with it (the film won the Grand Jury Prize) that he told Singer and his screenwriter Chris McQuarrie he wanted to be involved in their next project. Singer and McQuarrie–both *Wiseguy* fans–sent the *Suspects* script to the actor without telling him which part they wanted him to play.

Spacey actually appears to prefer selecting his film projects this way, as Amy Raphael noted during her 2002 interview with the actor: "He occasionally gets into trouble reading scripts, because he never asks which role the director has in mind."[249] Kevin subsequently called Singer and said he was interested in suave gang leader Keaton and Customs agent Kujan but also intrigued by Kint whom, it turned out, McQuarrie had written with the actor in mind; the fact that he and Kint's alter-ego share the same initials is surely no coincidence.

The physical description of Verbal in McQuarrie's original screenplay certainly evokes Spacey: "He has a deeply lined face, making his thirty-odd years a good guess at best."[250] "The dangers of ambition are what interest me," Spacey said in a contemporary interview with *Entertainment Weekly*. "I was driven to do *Suspects* because Verbal was more internal. It was a discipline for me to trust that stillness."[251]

The *Suspects* plotline is deceptively simple. Told in flashback, the film starts with the wounded Dean Keaton (Gabriel Byrne), alone on the deck of a ship. He is approached by a mysterious shadowed figure. "I can't feel my legs–Keyser," mumbles Byrne, as the other man raises a gun and appears to shoot him before dropping a match and setting the ship ablaze. There are only two survivors of the fire, a badly burned Hungarian mobster and crippled con artist Roger "Verbal" Kint, who is unharmed.

FBI agent Jack Baer (Giancarlo Esposito) interrogates the Hungarian, who claims that "Keyser Söze," a legendary Turkish crimelord, was responsible for the massacre in the harbour. The Hungarian begins to describe Söze while a translator interprets and a police sketch artist draws a rendering of Söze's face. Kint has already agreed to testify about the incident in exchange for full immunity, and is taken to a cramped, messy office by Dave Kujan (Chazz Palminteri) to be informally interrogated.

"New York–six weeks ago…" Five career criminals–Keaton, Kint, wild young McManus (Stephen Baldwin), sharply-dressed, unintelligible Fenster (Benicio Del Toro) and jovial smartass Hockney (Kevin Pollack)– are brought together for the police line-up that famously featured on promotional posters for the film.

Thrown into a shared cell, the quintet get acquainted, with McManus soon convincing the others to join forces to sting a group of corrupt cops running a fake courier service. A later con–ambushing a purported jewel dealer who turns out to be carrying heroin–brings the five to the attention of polite Pakistani lawyer Kobayashi (Pete Postlethwaite), who tells them that through their past activities all have been inadvertently involved in stealing from "Keyser Söze." Keaton, McManus, Fenster and Hockney are both shocked and awed by this revelation. Only Verbal asks: "Who's Keyser Söze?"

Now in Söze's debt, the group is ordered to attack a ship in San Pedro Harbor that is involved in a $91 million cocaine smuggling operation. Fenster wants out and is killed by Kobayashi; the remaining four agree to do the job to prevent the lawyer from murdering Keaton's girlfriend Edie (Suzy Amis). Keaton has grown fond of the puny Verbal–Spacey appears to have modelled his performance in their scenes alone together on Dustin Hoffman's "Ratso" Rizzo character from *Midnight Cowboy*–and attempts to shield him during the attack by leaving him concealed on the docks.

The raid, however, is a trap. Hockney and McManus are killed and Keaton discovers that there is no cocaine on the boat. Shot in the back, Keaton collapses, and the film returns to its opening scene as the concealed figure with the gun appears above him once again.

Back in the cluttered office, Kujan reveals what he believes to be the real purpose of the assault on the ship: to enable the murder of an Argentinean passenger aboard, one of the few individuals who could identify Söze. The Customs agent is convinced that Keaton faked his death and deliberately left Verbal alive only in order to confirm it to the authorities–Keaton *was* Keyser Söze.

His protector having been revealed as a manipulative coward, Verbal is a broken man. He shuffles tearfully out of the office as Kujan watches in sympathetic contempt. Turning to the bulletin board on the wall, Kujan realises that details and names from Kint's account of the raid are culled from articles pinned to it, and that the coffee cup he has been drinking from as he wandered around the room during the interrogation has "Kobayashi" stamped on the base.

Seemingly-guileless Verbal is revealed to have concocted the whole tale from information relating to other people–something Spacey himself has evidently had a lot of practice at. Kujan chases after Verbal, running past a fax machine as it receives the sketch artist's impression of Söze's face, which resembles–yup–Kevin Spacey. Kint/Söze is long gone: dropping his limp and straightening out his fingers as he moves along the sidewalk, he gets into a car driven by "Kobayashi" as the frantic Kujan searches in vain.

Collective gasp from the audience. The master of camouflage has pulled off his greatest con yet. "So many things that that movie said to me were beneath the surface," Spacey told his old classmate Mare Winningham in 1997. "It's a great thriller or mystery, but on another level it's a film about the fact that, if you only look at a person through one lens, or only believe what you're told, you can often miss the truth that is staring you in the face."[252]

Thanks to a clever pre-release marketing campaign from Gramercy Pictures, who plastered "Who is Keyser Söze?" posters over buses and billboards across the U.S., the film became one of the most highly-anticipated releases of the year. It premiered at the 1995 Sundance Film Festival and was shown out of competition at Cannes, then given an exclusive run in Los Angeles and New York City before going on wider release.

Critical reaction to the "diabolically clever" and "deliciously intricate"[253] movie was largely positive, audience reception almost universally so. *Suspects* was a hit at the box office, earning $23.5 million–against a budget of less than six–in North America alone. Singer was favourably compared to Quentin Tarantino, then the "hottest" young director in Hollywood after the success of his films *Reservoir Dogs* (1991) and *Pulp Fiction* (1994). The twist ending that reveals the rest of the film to be a fallacy–never an easy trick to pull on the viewer–was rarely derided as "a cop out" and Spacey, as both the key to the movie and the person with the most screen time, was particularly praised.

"In a top-flight company of actors, Mr. Spacey steals the film with his sly performance,"[254] commented Caryn James of *The New York Times*.

"Just for the record, *Suspects* is Spacey's show. It's Verbal's torrent of words, and the flickers of fear and cunning dancing in his stoolie eyes that keep us riveted…[His] balls-out brilliant performance is Oscar bait all the way… just the movie for an actor who's full of surprises,"[255] added a prophetic Peter Travers in *Rolling Stone*.

As actor Samuel L. Jackson–a friend of Spacey's since his early days in New York–observed in 1998: "[*Suspects*] could have been just another quirky film. Without Kevin, Keyser Söze doesn't work."[256] Much was made of the parallels between the "almost unknown" Spacey and the enigmatic Söze–though (as is borne out by this book!) the idea that Kevin was an overnight sensation is a somewhat false one.

By the time the Oscar nominations were announced in February 1996, Kevin had already received several awards for his portrayal of Kint/Söze, including a Best Supporting Actor gong from the Boston Society of Film Critics. The New York Film Critics Circle honoured not only his performance in *Suspects* but his three preceding roles in *Swimming With Sharks, Outbreak* and *Se7en* as well. "I think it's about time," Denis Leary, his co-star in *The Ref*, noted with regard to the Film Critics Circle nod. "[Kevin is] an incredibly talented, funny, creative, risky and generous actor."[257]

On 25th March 1996, Kevin Spacey–sporting a distinctive white tuxedo and a pair of cufflinks on "lucky loan" from eight-time nominee Jack Lemmon–attended the 68th Academy Awards ceremony at the Dorothy Chandler Pavilion in Los Angeles, accompanied by mother Kathleen as his "date." "I felt there was nobody else who deserved to share that evening more than her,"[258] Spacey later confirmed.

Kevin did not keep his teenage promise to take Randy to the Oscars too: by this time the relationship between the brothers had deteriorated to the extent that Kevin's next Thanksgiving communiqué to his elder sibling consisted of a still shot from the movie *L.A. Confidential* tersely signed: "For Randall, Glad to hear things are going well, Kevin." The picture came with a Post-It note from Kathleen (who disliked Randy telling associates that he was related to Kevin) stating: "For <u>home</u> only–do <u>not</u> put in office."[259]

The firm favourite to win Best Supporting Actor, Spacey duly received his dues and earned a chuckle from the audience as he accepted the statuette with the words: "Whoever Keyser Söze is, I can tell you he's going to get gloriously drunk tonight." Turning in Kathleen's direction, he added: "Thank you so much, Mom, for driving me to those acting classes on Ventura Boulevard when I was 16. I told you they would pay off."[260] Taking his mother to the Oscars, however, would garner media attention of another sort and thrust the spotlight on a place where, to Kevin's mind, it had no right to be: his private life.

# Chapter Eight
# Outing Spacey

*"Has he ever been married? The question elicits a long sigh, a nervous laugh and a cryptic answer: 'Oh...man...wow...I've been close.'"*
−*People Magazine* profile of Kevin Spacey (1991)[261]

*"It would sure be great if it didn't matter, but it does..."*
−Kevin Spacey's response to the question "Is it damaging for an aspiring leading man to be labeled gay?" in *Playboy Magazine* (1999)[262]

*"America isn't ready for the real me."*
−Jack Vincennes, *L.A. Confidential* (1997)

Whilst rumours about Kevin Spacey's sexuality had been circulating around Hollywood for years–a 1991 *People* profile of the actor even opened with the words "ROOTING AROUND IN THE CLOSET OF Kevin Spacey's career can be an unsettling task"[263]–it was not until 1997 that they really entered the public domain, courtesy of one Tom Junod and an *Esquire* story entitled "Kevin Spacey Has A Secret."

The front cover of the magazine set the tone, with a smug-looking Kevin pictured, arms folded, against a bright pink background. The article begins: "'Kevin Spacey?' my Mom said. 'I hear he's ...' I mean, my mother KNOWS. Or thinks she knows. Or supposes. Or suspects..."[264]

Junod uses the fact that Spacey was then filming a role as a gay man in the movie *Midnight in the Garden of Good and Evil* to blur the lines between actor and character. In *Midnight*, released in late 1997, Spacey plays Savannah antiques dealer Jim Williams, who is accused of murdering his young employee/lover Billy Hanson (Jude Law). Eventually found innocent of the crime, Williams dies of an apparent heart attack shortly after his acquittal in the room where he shot Hanson, while a bloodied ghost-Billy looks on: voodoo is one of the movie's major themes.

*Midnight* was loosely based on real life events, dramatized in journalist John Berendt's bestselling book of the same name. Berendt described Williams as possessing "darkly handsome, almost sinister features…eyes so black they were like the tinted windows of a sleek limousine–he could see out, but you couldn't see in"[265]: not exactly dissimilar to Spacey, then.

As was the case with many gay-themed Hollywood films from the Nineties–most famously the 1993 Tom Hanks starrer *Philadelphia*–Williams's homosexuality is "sanitised" for the screen. He is never shown being intimate with Billy or any other male (some additional scenes between Spacey and Law were cut from the final release print). Williams does however make one declaration of love for the youth, which Spacey delivers with real tenderness.

"Billy and I had a bond," he tells the Berendt character (John Cusack), "but that's not something that they're [the jury] ever going to understand. They'll just see the sex, and the age difference. But Billy was going to make something of himself. Great things–great people–can come from humble beginnings. He needed what I gave him, and I needed what he gave me. Now, you wish to pass judgement on that?" "No," answers Cusack softly.

Ever the committed artist, Spacey spent several weeks before filming commenced meeting with people who had known the real life Williams. As he told Junod: "The popular conception of Jim Williams in Savannah was that he was a sinewy, sinister, closeted, tortured homosexual into rough trade. In my research, I found a very different [person]. He was a southern gentleman. He was very at ease with his sexuality. He was not hidden, and I do not play him that way."[266] In his description of Spacey-as-Williams, however, Junod calls the actor "a creature of entrances and exits," alluding to both the metaphorical "closet" and the practice of homosexual intercourse, and states: "If he's learned anything, anything at all, from his life or his art, it's that he who keeps his secret the longest wins."[267]

The *Esquire* profile, composed as it was almost entirely of deliberately provocative, crude innuendo, offended gay and straight readers alike. Kevin's actual "secret" appears to be the fact he "wants to be a movie star," something that would have come as no surprise to Richard E. Grant and many others who had worked with the increasingly-dissatisfied Spacey in the early Nineties, yet Junod spends most of the piece teasingly implying that he is Suspected Of Being A Homosexual as if the word "gay" was akin to "paedophile": it was as if Stonewall and thirty years of liberation had never happened.

Through his publicist, Staci Wolfe, Spacey issued a statement calling the article "dishonest and malicious."[268] Prior to writing it, Junod had spent several days socialising with Kevin on the set of *Midnight,* accompanying the actor and some friends (who were unaware that he was a reporter) to restaurants and night-clubs around Savannah, where the film was shot: it's no wonder Spacey felt so betrayed. "*Esquire* has made it abundantly clear that they have now joined the ranks of distasteful journalism," he added, "and this mean-spirited, homophobic, offensive article proves that the legacy of Joseph McCarthy is alive and well."[269]

Spacey's agent at William Morris, Brian Gersh, said that he would advise his other clients not to grant interviews to *Esquire* as a result of their "deceptive and fraudulent behavior with respect to their interview with Kevin Spacey,"[270] while *Esquire* itself attempted to atone for the piece by naming Spacey one of the hundred most important people of the year in their next issue.

A half-hearted apology from Junod–in *The Advocate*, natch–grudgingly followed. "I did not expect to 'out' Kevin," he informed the magazine, "because I thought he *was* 'out.' I had heard so many people say, 'You know he's gay'–as the first or second thing that they said. Then I go out there, and suddenly it's a completely different thing."[271]

Curiously, Spacey did not take this opportunity to set the record straight (as it were). As he had told Junod during the interview, when the writer repeated his mother's "suspicions": "I live in a world in which I work with many different people all day long. They're my friends, and I *love* them. And many of these people *are* gay or homosexual. And I can't imagine feeling the need to jump up and say, 'I'm not one of them.' If anyone wants to think that, they're absolutely free to think that. I have no interest in confirming or denying that at *all*. It's just of no interest to me. So *what?*"[272]

Staci Wolfe was equally non-committal: "While Mr. Spacey respects many diverse life styles and admires those who have chosen to come out with dignity and courage, he has always maintained a separation between his professional and personal life, and will continue to do so. His decision not to publicly define his private life has apparently prompted this publication's attempt to present as fact their version of what they imagine his private life to be."[273]

Two years later, however, the wind had changed. Kevin's policy of non-disclosure up to that point was admirable, but there were whispers of another Oscar nod in the offing for *American Beauty*. The praise heaped upon the movie by film critics surpassed even that directed at *The Usual Suspects*. "A rich, brilliant and unnerving film, by far the strongest American film of the year,"[274] claimed *The New Yorker*, while *The New York Post* deemed it "a flat-out masterpiece,"[275] *The Independent* "a film touched by magic,"[276] *The Times* "just exquisite"[277] and *The News of the World* "as close to perfect as they come."[278]

Audiences seemed in agreement. *Beauty* had grossed over $350 million worldwide by the end of its theatrical run, a nifty return on the $15 million budget. As had also been the case with *Suspects*, while the rest of the ensemble cast gained favourable notices for their strong, vibrant performances, the actor with the most screen time was again singled out for special recognition.

"I make no apologies for putting Kevin Spacey's head slightly higher than the rest," gushed one reviewer. "The man is an acting genius who just gets better with every challenging role that he is not afraid to tackle–his sense of timing, his intonation, his knowing approach, his instinct; he is the consummate actor."[279] In the face of such acclaim, a prize from the Academy Award committee seemed almost assured, but for one pesky little thing...

The Hollywood attitude to homosexuality is a mix of contradictions. As campaigner and critic Vito Russo once pithily observed, the American film industry regards gay relations as "something you [do] in Europe or in the dark–preferably both."[280] Stars are encouraged to wear AIDS ribbons, support GLAAD[281] rallies, attend lavish parties thrown by Sir

Elton John—and leave their same-sex partners at home. Gay best friends are *de rigeur*, gay lovers are career cancer.

While it is "acceptable" for ancient character actors and behind-the-scenes personnel to be homosexual (or to be perceived as such), it is definitely NOT acceptable for leading men. *Playing* gay is a sure-fire way to earn an Oscar nomination, but no openly gay performer has ever taken the Best Actor Academy Award home, something which the erudite Spacey would have been well aware of.[282]

It seemed that affirmation of Kevin's hetero credentials was needed—and where better to display them than that bastion of healthy red-blooded-male fantasy, *Playboy Magazine*? In a classic piece of media manipulation worthy of Keyser Söze himself, Kevin not only denied outright that he was gay ("It's not true. It's a lie"), but claimed "the rumours" actually improved his sex life, with hordes of eager females flocking to "convert" him!

> **Playboy:** Has it affected your love life?
>
> **Spacey:** Most of the women I know haven't heard of the [*Esquire*] article. If they have, they know not to believe what they read. Then there are a few women who think the article might be true. It's a challenge for them: They want to be the ones to turn me around. I let them.
>
> **Playboy:** So you've managed to find a silver lining.[283]

The reaction from certain sectors of the gay press was as predictable as it was inevitable, as those who saw Spacey's denial as a "sell out"—the cryptic maverick finally stooping to play the Hollywood game—sifted frantically through the archives for contrary evidence. This rather snarky extract from *The New York Press's* "Tired Hedonist" column is fairly representative:

> "Ever since Kevin Spacey made it known a week or so ago that he is definitely heterosexual, at least one gay friend of mine—I'll call him 'Bill,' for that is his name—has been rather glum. It seems that Bill, a boyish-looking blond lawyer, was under the impression that Kevin Spacey had picked him up one night in the mid-80s in an East Village club called the Boy Bar, and that the two of them had

subsequently shared a tender moment at Bill's apartment. Now Bill knows that this 'Kevin Spacey' must have been an imposter, since the real Kevin Spacey is straight..."[284]

*Village Voice* columnist Michael Musto–who referred to Spacey's Oscar offensive as his "'I'm just wild about vagina' campaign"–was similarly arch: "How depressing! That means that all the people I know who've told me about guys Spacey's dated, done, or come on to are utter, complete liars with a reckless disregard for real life! I must stop hanging out with such disreputable, cowardly worms!"[285]

*Out Magazine's* response–with tongue firmly in cheek–was to dub Kevin one of the gay community's "straight allies" in their annual "Out 100" list. "His breathless confession in October's *Playboy*...just tickled us pink, pink, pink," Spacey's "dedication" read. "Brava, Kevin–we're so impressed."[286]

Supermarket tabloid *Star* got in on the act too, publishing several pictures of Spacey embracing and holding hands with a male companion in Oakland Memorial Park in Topanga, on the outskirts of Los Angeles. Spacey and Mr. X–the young man's face was obscured–had met up at a restaurant before driving to the park in the actor's Porsche Boxster. "The whole scene just screamed intimacy and togetherness...if my wife saw me with another man like that, she would be divorcing me,"[287] commented one observer who saw the pair together.

"Mr. Spacey will be pleased that we left out one or two images that were far more graphic," *Star's* editor, Tony Frost, gloated in an exchange with *The New York Daily News*. "We showed considerable restraint."[288] The tabloid's headline itself left little to the imagination: "Kevin Spacey Romps With Male Model! Amazing photos of Oscar winner's secret double life."

"Oscar winner," though: that was the key. Fortunately for Spacey, *Star* had gone to print too late to affect his Academy Award chances. *American Beauty*, as predicted, swept the board at the ceremony in L.A.'s Shrine Auditorium on 26th March 2000, winning in five of the eight categories in which it was nominated, including the prestigious Best Picture, Best Director and Best Original Screenplay, as well as Best Actor for the leading man.

Spacey attended the event accompanied, as ever, by his adoring mother, but this time there was a new girl in tow—script supervisor Dianne Dreyer, who rated a tender tribute in Kevin's acceptance speech ("thank you for teaching me about caring about the right things, and I love you") and, despite not having been seen in public with Spacey before, had apparently been dating him for several years.

Dreyer appears to be the woman referenced in a *Sunday Times Magazine* interview that Spacey gave in December 1999: "I've been in a stable relationship for a very long time, but she does not want to be known. We never wanted to be perceived as a couple, or even worse, as some kind of showbiz couple. We made a decision long ago that our lives would be private, but it got to a point where all our friends and family knew...It's not as if we'll be inviting *Hello!* into our home, but at least I will now acknowledge that she exists."[289]

Spacey's Wikipedia profile page notes that he was "discreetly" involved with Dreyer "from 1992 to 2000"[290]: from his comments in *Playboy* this was clearly not an exclusive union, however.[291] "Diane," the viperous Hollywood agent in Douglas Carter Beane's 2006 play *The Little Dog Laughed*, who engineers a marriage between her own closeted client, Mitchell, and Mitchell's secret lover's pregnant girlfriend, was supposedly named after Dreyer. Mitchell's and Spacey's heterosexuality-affirming award acceptance speeches are virtually identical, as "Diane's" opening monologue reveals:

> "As to his date to this award ceremony, he would like to bring his mother...I throw a flame retardant blanket on this potential brush fire, and volunteer myself as his date. I'm lesbian, he's a fag, we're in show business, we're a perfect couple...his acceptance speech is inspired...'To Diane,' my client states, significant tears finding their lazy way down his derma-braised face. 'The woman who taught me...how to love. And how...to dream.'"[292]

Though the *Star* affair would not be the last time that being caught unawares in a park would cause Kevin problems, the "romp" with the unknown young man did not rate a mention in many other tabloids–who chose instead to focus on the "safer" story of a possible romance between Spacey and his newly-divorced *Pay It Forward* co-star Helen Hunt, who reputedly accompanied her fellow Oscar winner on a vacation to the Caribbean–and appeared to be soon forgotten by the media at large.

Since winning his second Academy Award, Kevin has rarely spoken explicitly about his personal life, usually choosing, as he did before his *Beauty* Oscar campaign, not to discuss his romantic relationships at all. "I've just never believed in pimping my personal life out for publicity," he told a *Gotham* reporter in 2007. "I'm not interested in doing it. Never will do it."[293] While he has sometimes expressed a wish to become a father, he has not revealed whom he plans to have children with.[294]

Kevin has remained wary of another *Esquire*-style "set-up," once storming out of a planned appearance on Miami radio talk show *Power 96* when he discovered that drag artiste RuPaul (who cheekily dubbed him "Miss Spacey") was the guest DJ.[295] When *New York Magazine* published a short piece–entitled "Spacey out in Fire Island"–stating that the actor had hired a private villa in the predominantly-gay neighbourhood of Fire Island Pines for his 2002 August vacation,[296] Kevin's acerbic letter to the editor denying the story was almost three times as long as the original article itself.

"I have been far too busy this summer working at a small amusement park in Boise, Idaho, to find time to rent an expensive beach house anywhere," he stated, adding: "I have never been to Fire Island–not even as a visitor," before sneeringly closing the letter with: "P.S. I'm not really in Boise. Just in case you believe everything you read."[297]

A journalist who asked Kevin how he felt about "those stories about you being gay" during a press conference to promote *The Life of David Gale* in early 2003 provoked a similarly testy response. "Don't bother me with that crap," Spacey snapped. "Just mind your own f***ing business!"[298]

When a list of "Famous Gays and Lesbians" compiled by a U.K. government-sponsored LGBT group in 2005 as part of an information pack for schools was found to include Spacey, the organiser, Paul Patrick, was forced to revise the list: "We double check our material carefully but Mr. Spacey's name got through. I don't know how. It will be withdrawn. It should not have happened and we apologise."[299]

Whether the revision was made due to pressure from Kevin's management company is unclear, though the incident was certainly an embarrassment for the group and served to undermine their entire ethos: the "apology" demonised homosexuality almost as much as Tom Junod's *Esquire* article had. Kevin has stayed a favourite target amongst the LGBTQ community as the "butt of jokes"–as George Rush and Joanna Molloy mused after a Spacey roasting at a GLAAD dinner at the New York Hilton in 2001, "what gay and lesbian event would be complete without a little dig at Kevin Spacey?"[300]

It is interesting to consider how Kevin's enigmatic persona informs the roles he plays. The speculation about his own sexuality added a certain *frisson* to his brief kiss with Chris Cooper in *American Beauty*–while declaration of one's gay identity so often seals a character's fate, here it is Lester's *heterosexuality* that leads to his death.

Although *Midnight in the Garden of Good and Evil's* Jim Williams remains Kevin's only explicitly "gay" part to date, there are many queer intimations in other Spacey characters. Despite his notably deep voice, there's always been a trace of effeteness to the screen Spacey–"a malign femininity,"[301] as Lesley White of *The Sunday Times Magazine* termed it in 1999.

After conducting another 1999 interview with Kevin, Claire Armitstead pointed out "the strange feminine quality" in his acting. "Suddenly I can see why there has been so much speculation about his sexuality," she added, after watching Spacey state his passion for "his temple," the theatre. "It's a moment of pure, sardonic camp at the same time as being utterly serious… as if he's taking time out from a Stephen Sondheim musical."[302]

This quality is something Spacey has exaggerated for roles such as *Se7en's* softly spoken, bookish but nevertheless deadly John Doe. Kevin's Everyman looks–the killer is "John Doe by choice"–are employed in this movie to great effect. The film recounts a week in the lives of two detectives, the cultured, calm, about-to-retire William Somerset (Morgan Freeman) and his new partner, brash young David Mills (Brad Pitt), whose investigation into the death by force-feeding of an obese man leads them to the realisation that a serial killer is targeting those guilty of each of the seven deadly sins and making the "punishment" fit the "crime."

We first see the character of Doe–or his hands, at least–in a montage over the opening credits of the movie, cutting his fingertips with a razor and making tiny, meticulous notes with a felt pen in his journal. He appears again, Keyser Söze-like, as a distant figure in a fedora at the end of the corridor outside the apartment he rents, who draws a gun and fires at Mills before running away. Mills chases him into the street, where the shadowy Doe is again seen in long shot and midshots from behind as he runs across the road and is thumped by a car. There are also close-ups of his feet and gloved hands as he surprises Mills by hitting him on the head with an iron bar as the detective inches round the side of a stationary truck.

Doe's dark figure is reflected in a puddle as he raises a gun to Mills's head–echoes of the Subway Thief–and in one final, silhouetted close up before Somerset arrives on the scene and he flees. It is not clear from these small glimpses whether this is actually Spacey or a stand-in; however it is certainly Kevin who appears on the stairs leading to the apartment of the third victim, "Sloth," wearing a wig and glasses and affecting a high whiny voice in his disguise as a press photographer.

Doe's "true" entrance–one of the most memorable in movie history–occurs almost 91 minutes into the two-hour film. As Mills and Somerset walk along the street towards the police station, discussing the case–"either we'll get John Doe, or he'll finish his series of seven and this case will go on for years"–the camera pans past them to a halting yellow cab. A shaven-headed man emerges, filmed from the back as he follows Mills and Somerset into the station. For a few moments no-one notices him–despite the fact that he is covered in blood and his fingers are swathed in sticking plasters, it takes a loud cry of "Detective!" to gain Mills's attention.[303]

The mannered, artful Doe–one critic noted "he's like the world's most demonic sissy"[304]–is contrasted sharply with his eventual-killer Mills's brazen machismo (pretty-boy Pitt, unshaven and frequently bloodied around the face, has never looked less clean-cut than he does in *Se7en).* As Richard Dyer states in his British Film Institute guide to the film: "Kevin Spacey's performance, the rather prissy lips and precise delivery, the shot of him delicately dunking a tea bag in a cup after his arrest, might add up to a sense of Doe's effeminacy."[305]

*The Usual Suspects* has many similar touches. Verbal's coy "I like cops" to Kujan at the beginning of the interrogation is akin to Doe's droll "I didn't do that!" when a dead dog is found by the roadside as Mills and Somerset escort him to the supposed location of his last two victims' bodies. "In the end," BFI author Ernest Larsen said of *Suspects*, "Kevin Spacey's performance is ambiguous enough to suggest that Verbal is infatuated with Keaton."[306]

And Spacey can be even more subtle–what other actor could have brought such a tormented edge to Jack Vincennes? Dressed in sunglasses and a succession of snappy blazers, the epitome of Hollywood cop cool–director Curtis Hanson told Spacey to "think Dean Martin"[307]–Jack is the Big Kahuna of his LAPD division in the 1950s-set *L.A. Confidential* (1997). When we first meet Jack he is dancing with a woman[308] at a party, however after a brief spin around the floor they part and Jack remains romantically unattached, seemingly immune to the fascination for starlet Lynn Bracken (Kim Basinger) that infects his colleagues Bud White (Russell Crowe) and Ed Exley (Guy Pearce).

As well as serving as a "technical adviser" for *Dragnet*-style TV show *Badge of Honor*, Jack is on the payroll of opportunistic journo Sid Hudgens (Danny DeVito), trapping a young pair of contract players in a pot-fuelled clinch early on in the film for the other man to photograph. Jack later sees one of the actors, "AC/DC and broke" Matt Reynolds (Simon Baker)[309] on the *Badge of Honor* set and persuades the desperate youth to "be nice" to a closeted district attorney in order that Sid can burst in on them at an intimate moment and get the scoop.

There is a distinct chemistry between Spacey and Baker in their second brief scene together, and Jack has a rare attack of conscience over tricking the young man. Sitting alone in a bar (incongruously called the Frolic Room), watching his reflection in the full-length mirror, he makes a decision that will seal his own fate. Laying the blood money from Sid across his glass, he heads off to the D.A.'s motel room but finds Reynolds dead on the floor.

Spacey's expressive eyes have rarely been used to better effect. In one single, agonised close-up as he crouches beside the body, his reactions–"a kind of tender despair,"[310] as Manohla Dargis notes in her guide to the film–delicately suggest that Vincennes recognises a hitherto-concealed part of himself in the murdered boy. Jack's determined to find the truth about his death, telling Exley that "There's a case you boys in Homicide don't care about…they think it's just another Hollywood homo-cide, but I don't."

Enlisting the support of boss Dudley Smith (James Cromwell), however, proves to be a mistake. "I messed something up–I'm trying to make amends," Jack tells him during a late-night visit to the latter's home. "Don't start trying to do the right thing, boyo," Dudley cautions. "You haven't had the practice." Jack acknowledges this with a wry smile.

After establishing that Jack has not yet passed his latest suspicions about Reynolds's murder on to Exley, Smith suddenly pulls out a gun and shoots him through the heart as he sits at his dinner table. The death of Jack Vincennes is truly shocking, as unexpected as Spacey's gory arrival in *Se7en* and played brilliantly by the actor as he remains in frame for several seconds after the shooting (he asked director Curtis Hanson to paint two black dots on the wall by Cromwell's head to provide him with the correct focus point).

"People have asked whether I did something CGI in the lab, because you literally see the light go out in his eyes. It was not only live, it was one take. I was standing next to the camera and couldn't believe it,"[311] Hanson revealed in 2002. The added poignancy provided in the earlier scenes with Baker brings Jack a redemption that is absent from James Ellroy's source novel, where he is shot in the face during a gunfight in one of the final chapters of the book.

Ellroy himself was impressed: "This is a deep immersion performance. It's some of the best self-loathing I've ever seen on screen. [Spacey is] only on screen I'd say half as much as Pearce or Crowe, and he steals every scene he's in because there's something going on internally, and your eyes automatically shift to him."[312] *American Beauty* director Sam Mendes once made a similar observation: "He has a laser beam behind his eyes. With just a twitch of the head he zaps you and makes the hairs stand up on the back of your neck."[313]

As Janet Maslin of *The New York Times* observed: "Mr. Spacey is at his insinuating best, languid and debonair, in a much more offbeat performance than this film could have drawn from a more conventional star"[314] (scruffy Kiefer Sutherland, who played Vincennes in a TV pilot filmed in 1999, effectively conveyed Jack's cynicism but little else: the show failed to attract enough interest to be turned into a full series).

"What is special about Kevin is his combination of slyness, mischievousness and superior intelligence–a combination not a lot of actors have," Hanson said in 1999. "I want to see Kevin reveal those parts of himself, because that's what he is."[315] Tom Junod noted in his *Advocate* interview that "[Hanson] told me that after he cast Kevin, the executives said, 'You know he's gay, don't you?' He answered, 'Whether he is or isn't, it's good for the film, because he's playing a man with whom not all is as it seems.'"[316]

Spacey's ability to suggest great inner turmoil through a minimum of outward action–he himself described Jack as "a guy with the vibrato and the surface and the ring-a-ding, but something underneath deeply unsatisfied, like a volcanic charge that had to break"[317]–could perhaps be compared to that of an Anthony Perkins, or a Montgomery Clift–men of mystery both.

So what exactly is Spacey's orientation? His name has been linked to actor Stephen Geoffreys–and actress Sandra Bullock.[318] He's been photographed embracing men–and kissing women. His mom was his date at the 2000 Oscars, but he took a girlfriend too.

Even Kevin's closest friends swear ignorance of his "true" preferences. Duncan Weldon told *The Observer* in 2004 that "I don't know much about him on that front and I've never known him have a partner. I have seen him out with women, but I wouldn't like to tell you he was out socially... It never comes up in conversation. I wouldn't want to make a bet on his sexuality."[319] Linda Fiorentino, Spacey's *Ordinary Decent Criminal* co-star, once remarked that "Kevin has a sexuality that's subtle–beneath the surface."[320]

Maybe the last word should go to Kevin himself. His declaration to brother Randy during their Christmas 1987 heart-to-heart that "I don't consider myself heterosexual, homosexual or bisexual…I'm just sexual"[321] is classic Spacey, refusing to be pigeonholed by mere labels.

"To me, sex is a perfectly natural thing," says Jim Williams in *Midnight*, "just an occasional natural occurrence between consenting adults"–no doubt Kevin (who once quipped to a group of drama students that the best thing about the acting business was simply "the sex")[322] would agree. As he told *Empire Magazine* in 2000 in reference to the *Playboy* piece: "I thought, 'Well, maybe it's time. If I'm not going to tell people what I am, maybe it's time to tell people what I'm not'…The funny thing is now there are writers that say I'm, 'Loudly Protesting My Straightness.' A lot of other people are, 'Loudly Protesting My Straightness,' but I'm not. It's really no big deal."[323]

Spacey's mystique actually enhances his romantic appeal. William Leith noted whilst interviewing Spacey for *The Guardian* in 2002 that "Women have told me that they find his sexual ambiguity attractive, in a way they might not if they believed him to be either definitely gay or definitely straight."[324] Ironically, Hollywood's most elusive star–who was once described as "the thinking person's sex symbol"– has become its most accessible fantasy man. His "just sexual" persona excludes no one. We are all in with a chance…

# Chapter Nine

# Lost in Spacey

*"I used to see my mug in dailes and groan. Now I see it and think, 'Hey, you look like an aging Chinese character actress, AND THEY STILL HIRE YOU!'"*
–Kevin Spacey (1996)[325]

*"This is the highlight of my day. I hope it's not all downhill from here..."*
–Kevin Spacey on accepting his Oscar for *American Beauty* (2000)

Best Actor Oscar for the year's Best Film–what more could Kevin Spacey achieve now? What dizzy cinematic heights were left for him to scale? The answer, sadly, appeared to be: very few. Much is made of the "Oscar curse," under which performers who have been awarded the golden statuette find that projects on offer following a win are decidedly inferior to those on offer before it. As *Wiseguy's* Mel Profitt once remarked: "When you're standing on top of Everest there's only one direction left."

Let's get one thing clear, though. Kevin Spacey is not Tom Hanks. If Tom Hanks is your average-joe Good Fella, Mr. All-America, Spacey is somewhere out in the Atlantic. Tom does warm, Kevin does icy. Tom does sincere, Kevin does sly. Tom does cute pooch, Kevin does slippery snake. If the Eden serpent had hailed from New York, it would have sounded like Kevin Spacey.

"David Gale" was a Tom Hanks role.

Prior to landing the lead in *American Beauty*, Kevin Spacey had primarily been known for his character parts, either playing one of an ensemble (*The Usual Suspects, A Time To Kill, L.A. Confidential, Hurlyburly*), as part of a double-act with another main (male) actor (*Swimming With Sharks, Midnight in the Garden of Good and Evil, The Negotiator*), or lending quirky support to the "official" stars (*Se7en, Outbreak*).

After *Beauty*, he moved into more conventional "leading man" roles, often being seriously miscast in parts that seemed to call for the more pedestrian appeal of a Costner or a Gibson or a Cruise. Spacey was once described by the playwright Lanford Wilson as "medium everything"[326]—a phrase which captures his blend-into-the-background, Everyman look perfectly. His features are the ultimate "blank canvas," as Jerry Stahl noted in a 1996 profile: "Viewed one way, they look perfectly normal. Viewed another, his very averageness seems so extreme, so hypernaturally bland, as to render him terrifying. It's a composite of a hundred other faces. Keyser Söze and Verbal Kint rolled into one. The perfect mask for an actor."[327]

Terence Blacker observed in a 2004 article that "[Spacey's face] is not particularly beautiful or unusual; it is a face of natural, intelligent curiosity, one whose features have been interestingly etched by experience, good and bad."[328] In a contemporary review of *The Ref*, John Lyttle said: "Exciting and dangerous though he is, Kevin Spacey will never be a front-rank film star: there's something a mite too mean in that pig-cum-pug face and beefy body. A demon inhabits him, a demon that takes no prisoners and tells no lies. It's the sort of quality Hollywood allows only character actors to flaunt (Elisha Cook Jnr and Hope Emerson spring to mind) though there's always the exception that proves the rule: Jack Nicholson."[329]

As Spacey himself has conceded: "I am not a movie star in the sense that Brad Pitt is. I am just not that guy. And I had to fight and work hard to carve that career in film."[330] Lacking both the chiselled good looks of the classic romance player and the rugged machismo of the shoot-'em-up action hero, Kevin endured a rough couple of years on Hollywood's fickle wheel of fortune, starring in one critically panned flop after another.

"Just what the hell happened to Kevin Spacey's career?" asked Jonathan Ross in mid-2002. "A couple of years back he was at the very top of the tree...Since [*American Beauty*] he's made a lot of weird choices...He's gone from being a must-see actor to getting dangerously close to the must-avoid-like-the-plague category in about three years, which is surely a record of some kind."[331]

"His resolve to be mainstream, a nice guy or a romantic lead is by now as obstinate as it is fatuous," observed David Thomson in his 2003 biographical film guide. "It's like asking Lassie to be treacherous…"[332] Spacey was even included in *Esquire Magazine's* 2003 list of the "100 most overrated things on the planet," along with football pundit Des Lynam, Elvis Presley, Liverpool F.C., yoga, baked beans and Prozac!

"Kevin Spacey's films: now, usually suspect,"[333] sneered Renee Graham of *The Boston Globe* in a typical appraisal of the actor's post-*Beauty* turkeys, which included the sickly-sweet, mawkish *Pay It Forward* (2000), mediocre other-worldy drama *K-Pax* (2001), far-from-*Brokeback Mountain's*-league E. Annie Proulx adaptation *The Shipping News* (2001),[334] and the aforementioned hysterical, ludicrously-plotted *The Life Of David Gale* (2003), which might have stood a chance with the ever-amiable Hanks in the lead but with Spacey's fundamentally chilly persona was doomed from the start.[335]

The eponymous "hero" of *David Gale* is an active opponent of capital punishment who now awaits execution himself for the murder of a colleague. Spacey (who was the third choice to play Gale, after George Clooney and Nicolas Cage had both turned the part down) actually shot the film in late 2001, and subsequently took a year and a half off from acting to focus on his Trigger Street responsibilities and to spend some additional time with his close friends and family.

"I'd become somewhat ubiquitous," Kevin said. "And if I was sick of me, I could only imagine how the rest of the country was feeling…"[336] The film's director, Sir Alan Parker, later commented that Spacey was "rather unusual, in that he's the only actor I've worked with in 30 years who didn't give a toss whether I liked [the last take] or not."[337]

Like *Swimming With Sharks* and *The Usual Suspects*, *David Gale* is told in a series of flashbacks (even using brief visual collages of keywords such as "Lust" and "Self-Sacrifice" to introduce each new scene in a naff homage to *Se7en*). With four days to go before his date with the needle, Gale agrees to tell his story to ambitious young journalist Elizabeth "Bitsey" Bloom (played by Kate Winslet in full Girl's Own mode).

A philosophy professor at the (fictional) University of Austin, Gale was targeted by one of his students, Berlin (Rhona Mitra) who had recently failed his class, leading to her expulsion. After seducing the drunken Prof at a party (the bathroom sex scene between Spacey and the Angela-wannabe—"No–from behind! Do it hard! Bite my shoulder!"–is probably his most cringe-inducing filmic moment ever), she falsely accused him of rape.

Although Berlin later dropped the charges, the resulting scandal cost David both his job and his marriage, and he began to drink heavily. After his wife left him, he grew close to Constance Harraway (Laura Linney), a fellow activist from the group Deathwatch, and was the prime suspect when she was found raped and murdered, a plastic bag tied round her head and her hands cuffed behind her back.

As Bloom discusses the Harraway death with Gale, it becomes clear that the facts do not add up—"Someone's framing you?" she exclaims. Bitsey subsequently finds a videotape of the dying Constance in her motel room that suggests Gale has indeed been incriminated, leaving the plucky journo only one more day to solve the mystery (Yikes!) and save poor David from execution.

After Bitsey attempts to re-enact Constance's death, she realises that Harraway actually recorded herself committing suicide. Stricken with leukaemia, the activist carried out her own personal "mercy killing." Bitsey goes to the home of Dusty Wright (Matt Craven), the mysterious ex-Deathwatch member who has been stalking her throughout the movie, and finds a fuller copy of the video which confirms her suspicions.

In a frenzy, Bloom struggles by car, and then by foot (her unreliable rental vehicle predictably breaks down), to present the evidence to stop the execution. Unfortunately, she doesn't reach the courthouse in time (Boo!), and finds that Gale has already expired. The tape is duly made public, resulting in a media and political uproar and, of course, providing opponents of the death penalty with a great ethical victory.

In an epilogue, Bloom receives a package in her office containing David's son's toy sheep: hidden inside is a videotape labelled "Off the Record." This shows Dusty standing over Harraway's body and confirming her death–then stepping aside to allow Gale to leave his thumb print on the plastic bag which Constance used to suffocate herself. The three of them–possibly in collusion with Gale's "inept" lawyer–had (shock!) scrupulously planned the whole thing.

"The first time that I read the script," Spacey told *Cinema Confidential* shortly before the movie opened, "I was confounded by it, I was confused by it, I was disturbed by it..."[338] So was the audience: unlike the surprise reveal at the end of *The Usual Suspects*, the climax of *David Gale* is one twist that manifestly does not work. Kevin's performance throughout is stilted and unsympathetic–for one critic "the most unwatchable by an Academy Award winner since Robin Williams' notoriously sappy portrayal of the titular character in [1998's] *Patch Adams*"[339]–and he thus fails to convince us that Gale possesses sufficient moral fibre to die for his beliefs.

In a contemporary critique, *The Daily Mail's* Christopher Tookey noted: "Spacey can be a fine actor, especially in roles which exploit his obvious intelligence, but he can't do warmth or pathos."[340] This Achilles' heel of Spacey's–perhaps his only shortcoming as a performer–is also apparent in *The Shipping News*, where Kevin's servile schlub is irritating rather than appealing.

As one *Shipping News* reviewer observed: "Spacey exudes malevolent urbanity like no other contemporary actor. However, he does not manage blank victimhood quite so well. In fact, Spacey's Quoyle is not so much a case of casting against type as of a superb actor casting his talents to the wind."[341] "Is this the same man whose silken menace lit up the screen a few years ago in *Se7en* and *L.A. Confidential*?" asked another former admirer. "Yes, I'm afraid it is, and where he once jangled our nerves, at present he just grates on them."[342]

As bad as *David Gale* was–the critics had a field day rubbishing its "fatal flaws," "deadly errors," "poor execution" and "missed penalties," with one wag noting the movie was "currently dying a quiet death at the American box office"[343]–it is hard to fault Kevin for wishing to extend his range, for wanting to play a character who wasn't Satan in human form.[344]

His oft-cited fear of "languishing"[345] in the same tired roles–another legacy of his nomadic childhood perhaps–and his perfectionist streak would have left him unsatisfied with only acting Machiavellian. A mere month after his second Oscar triumph, at least one reviewer was already urging Spacey in this direction:

"I hope he puts aside the projects that always seem to come to him first, the ones with the pages of attitude and arch dialogue and flip, hip edginess. I hope that for once, instead, he goes after the sort of projects that don't have an obvious 'Kevin Spacey part.' Scripts about decent, simple, inarticulate guys. Scripts about guys who aren't always the brightest bulb in the room, but still struggle, and manage to muddle through and maybe even occasionally come out on top."[346]

"It's absolutely intentional," Kevin said in February 2002. "I am absolutely not trying to do what I did five years ago. Does that mean I'll never do it again? No. If somebody writes a script as good as I got five years ago maybe I'll think about doing it. Most of the scripts that I read where there are characters of that darker side really just pale by comparison to a *Usual Suspects* or those kind of roles. So why bother to do some cheap version of something that I have done before and had an enormous amount of personal success doing?"[347] It's just unfortunate that the projects Kevin chose to explore his "good fella" persona with were so poor.[348]

Not that being a bona fide Leading Man changed Spacey much. Public Kevin is more often seen in old jeans and a baseball cap than a tux-and-tails. He seems as happy with a $5 deli sandwich and vanilla latte as a $5000-a-head exclusive feast at Spago. On location, he's more likely to request a pack of Marlboro Lights than a forty-foot Winnebago or a personal chef for his pet pooch.[349] He rarely travels with an entourage or even an assistant, eschewing limousines and private jets in favour of his trusty Zappy scooter, and there's no plastic surgeon on *his* payroll: you just know Kevin would never Botox.

"I don't want to live in a world where someone buys my clothes and lays them out and tells me what to wear," he said in 2001. "I do most things myself. I take my dry cleaning to the dry cleaners, and I enjoy doing it. I think that part of it is just the way I am, and another part of it is very calculated in the sense that I don't want to lose contact with the very thing that I should be in touch with all the time, which is life."[350]

Many of Spacey's fellow thespians have praised his commitment, lack of pretension, and wry sense of humour–often the icebreaker on the tense environment of a film or theatre set. Welsh actress Lisa Palfrey, who co-starred with Spacey on the London stage in *The Iceman Cometh*, later recollected: "It was a pleasure watching him act–he was so natural...he was very down to earth...we all shared dressing rooms–the boys had one and the girls had another, and he just mucked in with everyone."[351]

*L.A. Confidential's* Russell Crowe found his co-star "the most charming man. He's the Oscar Wilde of our time...He's always very open and effusive. His interest in you is genuine."[352] Irish actor Billy Carter, who appeared with Kevin in *A Moon for the Misbegotten* at the Old Vic, noted that "he really takes care of you and I have learned an awful lot from him,"[353] while *The Ref's* Judy Davis simply summarised Spacey as "terribly funny, very smart, very generous."[354] Iain Softley, who helmed *K-Pax*, said of the actor that "He's a real life force. Kevin has an incredible appetite–but he's very focused...I wish I could be that way."[355]

Kevin himself has claimed that he tries to model his on-set conduct on his mentor Jack Lemmon's, having observed the older actor during the filming of *Dad* contentedly completing the *New York Times* crossword in his tiny motorhome, the door wide open to admit all comers. "He exemplified the way you should treat the people around you–always making sure your co-workers feel important and confident, and are having an enjoyable experience. [Being an actor] elevates you into a position of responsibility because everyone around you looks to you as a leader."[356]

"Before I go to work," Spacey said in 1999, "I make it very clear what kind of environment I want on the set. If the integrity is being punctured by individuals, no matter what their position, I call a meeting and tell them that if they persist in bullying the PA or the caterer, I will not be coming back"[357] (Kevin was presumably being ironic when he told co-star Pete Postlethwaite on the set of *The Shipping News* that he needed two trailers because "with Hollywood–well, it's what you have if you want them to respect you. The extra one's for my make-up.")[358]

Spacey is also known for his consideration towards his followers. Betsy Model, who interviewed Kevin on the *David Gale* set, observed him as he was surrounded by university students, some of whom appeared as extras in the movie, during a break:

"Actor Kevin Spacey is simply Kevin to his fans…[he] appears to work hard to maintain that approachability, gladly spending 30 minutes or more signing notebooks and T-shirts, video boxes and photographs. He shakes hands, questions individuals on their majors and career aspirations, poses for snapshots, makes quips and jokes, and generally engages in light conversation with a couple [of] hundred people who want to say they've conversed with Kevin."[359]

As one shrewd British journalist noted in 2004: "You would be happy to be seated next to Kevin at a dinner party and would soon be telling him all sorts of stuff about your life and probably, out of politeness and good breeding, he would be adding a bit of stuff of his own to make you feel at ease…In a world where those cursed with fame so often prove to be egotistical nutters, he gives every appearance of being a relatively normal person."[360] Upon being asked during a 2006 interview how he "kept his ego in check," Spacey revealed that he has a photograph of himself on his desk taken during his Juilliard days, pointing at a piece of graffiti that reads: "Please kill me before I become famous!"[361]

However, even Mr. Casual has demonstrated occasional outbursts of diva-like behaviour. In late 1998 Spacey was cast as cocky career crook Michael Lynch in the film *Ordinary Decent Criminal* (which was not released in cinemas until March 2000, after Spacey had received his second Oscar nomination).[362] Modelled on real-life Irish crimelord Martin Cahill, Lynch is "married" to two sisters (played by Helen Baxendale and Linda Fiorentino) and has several children with them.

When he isn't spending time with his family, Michael is plotting heists with his gang. His brazen, stylish robberies make him the bane of the Gardaí (the Irish police force) and a folk hero among his working class Dublin community. "This thing of me becoming a bit of a TV star lately," Spacey (with cod-Oirish accent) says coolly to his posse, donning a pair of shades, "I want you all to know–it's not going to change me–one–little– bit…we're top of the ratings, lads. They might even give us our own series!"

While Lynch is very much a "man of the people," a certain American actor apparently was not. Scottish actor/director Peter Mullan, who played gang member Stevie, was initially enthused to be working with him. As he told *The Sun* just prior to production: "I'm waiting to start filming with Kevin Spacey for *Ordinary Decent Criminal*...Kevin is producing this film and he really loved [Mullan's previous movie] *My Name Is Joe*. It was the first time I've never had to audition."[363]

Relations between the two soon soured, however, and Mullan later recalled his co-star insisting on "VIP treatment" at all times:

> "I should have stuck one on him. I regret now that I did not. I remember him hiring two Range Rovers, in lilac, one for himself and the other to act as a decoy. He honestly believed there would be mass recognition. We did try to explain to him that we were in a city where Bono can walk down the street and nobody bothers him. Dubliners are not impressed by celebrities. He used to run around in a cap and dark glasses. He would always, wherever we went, take them both off with a flourish with the words 'Look who I really am.' But he got completely and absolutely no reaction."

Mullan also found Spacey's on-set behaviour difficult. "He is combative and the edge is always there. We had a set-to one day because he was not around to rehearse. We had to work with a stand-in. I finally said, 'No, let's wait until he arrives.' He came on and we had this silent thing going on. I thought, 'Go on—say something. I will take your gullet and rip it through your f****** heart.' I was really angry. We should have had it out. I was on the phone to my wife, saying, 'Tomorrow I am going to go crazy.' And she was saying, 'No—think of the money.' That job was the most I have been paid, but I will never take a job for the money again."[364]

Fellow Scot David Hayman, another cast member, revealed in a 2001 interview that the three-month shoot "wasn't a terribly pleasant experience. Kevin has got his own problems."[365] Six years later, he described the American actor as "an egotistical "w****r."[366] Even dialogue coach Brendan Gunn was irked: "[Kevin] didn't want to do the Dublin accent, so he didn't work at it, which was frustrating...I think Kevin is the only person I've ever been disappointed with."[367]

Nor was this the only project on which Spacey had his detractors. When making the film *Pay It Forward* in 2000, the actor managed to offend screenwriter Leslie Dixon, who eventually resigned from the production over his (and co-star Helen Hunt's) ungracious attitude.

"Immediately, Kevin let me know my caste," Dixon claimed in 2006. "During our first meeting, he made phone calls, without ever saying 'Excuse me,' or acknowledging that a person was sitting there. I was wallpaper…Occasionally, I was yelled at; more often, ignored. No one said a personal word to me–even knee-jerk courtesies like 'hello' and 'goodbye' had gone by the wayside. I quit."[368]

None of which boded well for the film Spacey had often described as his "dream project," a biopic of Sixties crooner Bobby Darin, which he had been shopping around Hollywood circles for years, trying to obtain funding for. Darin was a childhood hero of Kevin's ("By the time I was ten or 11, I was singing Bobby Darin hits into a hairbrush,"[369] he confessed in one interview) as well as one of mother Kathleen's favourite singers.

"She thought he was the greatest thing that ever walked the face of the earth, and I grew up in a house where Bobby Darin was playing all the time," Spacey told *IGN Magazine* shortly before the film's release. "I heard they were making a movie, or trying to make a movie [about Darin] at Warner Brothers, this is now the late '80s. I thought, 'This is the part for me. I'm born to play this part. I've got to play this part!' Unfortunately, they didn't think so…I began to work in film and television and every single year, at least three times a year, my manager would call over to Warner Brothers and say, 'Hey, what's happening with that Bobby Darin movie? You guys ever going to make it? Kevin really wants to do it.'"[370]

"I was got into music through my Dad's collection of big band and jazz 78s…Bobby did the same thing except he was singing to Frank Sinatra records,"[371] Spacey revealed in another interview. Producer Arthur Friedman, a long-time friend of Bobby's, bumped into Spacey in a Santa Monica shopping mall in 1995 and was struck by his resemblance to Darin. "I called [director] Barry Levinson but he said that Spacey–who had just made *The Usual Suspects*–just wasn't box office. He wanted Johnny Depp,"[372] Friedman recalled in 2004.

After the planned Levinson adaptation fell through, Spacey acquired the rights to Darin's story himself. Paramount agreed to finance the film, but had one proviso: Leonardo di Caprio as Darin! Spacey demurred. He was offered the part of sleazy lawyer Billy Flynn in the upcoming big-screen adaptation of the musical *Chicago,* but turned it down to focus on the Darin project, securing distribution through Lions Gate Entertainment.

Kevin took vocal training lessons from jazz artist Roger Kellaway, Darin's former accompanist, in order to convince Bobby's son Dodd and former manager Steve Blauner that he could reproduce the singer's voice accurately, and ended up not only playing Bobby in the released film, titled *Beyond the Sea,* but also directing, co-writing and co-producing it.[373]

*Beyond the Sea* was the second film Spacey had directed, the first being taut hostage drama *Albino Alligator* (1997). *Albino,* which starred Matt Dillon, Faye Dunaway and Gary Sinise, was shot in sequence on a $5 million budget and used only minimal sets (most of the action takes place in a small tavern named Dino's Last Chance Bar where three cons on the run take the patrons captive)–a complete contrast to the brightly surreal milieu of *Beyond the Sea.* Wary of dominating the production, Spacey ensured that–a Hitchcockian cameo apart–there would be no part for himself in the cast.

*Albino* did not fare well at the box office (Dunaway even "earned" a Razzie nomination as Worst Supporting Actress), but the film received some positive reviews which favourably compared it to both *Reservoir Dogs* and *The Usual Suspects,* and Spacey's confident and dynamic direction was also praised. As Janet Maslin noted in a contemporary review:

> "Mr. Spacey's cool, measured acting style is much in evidence anyway, since he directs this debut feature with an emphasis on interesting mannerisms very much like his own…He even achieves an unexpectedly elegant effect with a body that goes flying out the windshield of one car, landing in slow motion on the car in front of it."[374]

While Kevin was initially reluctant to direct *Beyond the Sea*, he took the helm after being unable to find anyone else suitable in time. *Beyond* chronicles sickly-kid-from-the-Bronx Walden Robert Cassotto's determined quest to rise from his working class Italian-American roots and become a bigger star than his idol Sinatra, supported all the way by his adoring Mom Polly (Brenda Blethyn). The film weaves fantasy sequences with scenes containing somewhat fictionalised versions of events in Darin's life (probably a wise move, given Spacey's age–Darin died at 37).

The screen Bobby is himself preparing to star in an autobiographical movie, and the adult singer frequently interacts with a young boy (played by William Ullrich in unappealing snotty-brat mode) who is both the "real" younger Bobby and the child actor playing him in Bobby's film. A slide in the end credits bears the coda: "This film is not a literal telling of the life of Bobby Darin. It is a creative work based on fact, but in dramatising the story for the screen some characters, events, dialogue and chronology have been fictionalised and of course, much has been left out."

Inspired to amend his name by a malfunctioning Chinese restaurant sign ("Mandarin"), "Bobby" lands a contract with Atlantic Records and enjoys teen idol success with "Splish Splash." Not wanting to limit his artistic potential, however, canny "Bob" changes his niche to big band singing and records classics such as "Mack the Knife." He also pursues a film career, earning an Oscar nomination for his role in *Captain Newman, M.D.* (1963), and romances and marries teenage actress Sandra Dee (Kate Bosworth).

As Bobby's success takes him on the road and away from home more often, Dee becomes addicted to alcohol. The couple separate, reconcile for long enough to produce son Dodd, then divorce (though they share several gooey "still-in-love" scenes afterwards). When Darin becomes involved in the campaign to elect Robert Kennedy as President and contemplates a political career of his own, his "sister" Nina (played by Caroline Aaron as a trashy loudmouth) delivers some shocking news. His beloved mother, now deceased, was actually his grandmother and he is Nina's illegitimate child, the son of an unidentified boy she dated in high school.

Devastated, Darin becomes a recluse, living in a trailer on the Big Sur coast in California. Out-of-step with changing music trends, he tries to adapt by incorporating folk music and protest songs into his repertoire, but finds himself rejected by his former fans. He decides to stage a gospel choir show at the Flamingo Hotel in Las Vegas, where he performs his new material in the style of the old hits that made him famous.

Against all odds, it's a huge success, but Darin's triumph is short-lived as he is rushed to hospital suffering from blood poisoning (his heart was weakened by rheumatic fever in childhood). The ending is pure invention: after seeming to die during surgery, the elder Bobby meets his younger self once again and, accompanied by a phalanx of male dancers, the two duet on "As Long as I'm Singing." Little Bobby disappears and a re-energised Big Bobby continues the song alone into the closing credits.

*Beyond the Sea* was released in December 2004 and proved a failure at the box office, making back less than $9 million of its $24 million budget. Whilst well-received by Darin's relatives, it was unpopular with many reviewers who disliked the "whitewash" of Darin's character: a case of Spacey taking his "good guy" act a step too far, perhaps?

Both Darin's son Dodd and Darin biographer David Evanier saw several similarities between the two men. "You can put Kevin's obsessiveness about getting the film made right up there with Bobby's obsessiveness," Evanier asserted. "He's also the ideal person to play Bobby. He has an uncanny physical resemblance to him, and he also has Bobby's intensity and dark side. Bobby had all this rage going on inside him. You can see that same volatile mix in Kevin's work as an actor, the way he can conjure up anger and ambivalence. Look at him in *Swimming With Sharks*."[375]

While this "dark side" may well have been part of the real-life Bobby, it is not apparent in the finished version of *Beyond the Sea*. Darin's relationship with Dee is far too romanticised to seem realistic,[376] his legendary womanising is scarcely mentioned (second wife Andrea is not referenced at all, nor is Darin's penchant for holding orgies) and his often-aggressive ambitious drive[377] comes across as quirky rather than cruel–"He may be an asshole, but he's our asshole," chant Bobby's "people" early in the movie.

Kevin was criticised for being too old for the role (there is a hefty 24-year age gap between himself and then-21-year-old co-star Bosworth, who is four years younger than *American Beauty's* Mena Suvari, while the real-life gap between Dee and Darin was eight years at most),[378] though his masterly duplication of Darin's singing voice was praised. His spirited performances of "Hello Young Lovers," "That's All" and the title track, as well as his poignant rendition of "The Curtain Falls" at Bobby's final concert, certainly enliven the movie and give a tantalising glimpse of what might have been had he played Darin at thirty.

Mick LaSalle of *The San Francisco Chronicle* was one of his harshest detractors. *"Beyond the Sea* is jaw-droppingly awful, a misbegotten and ill-conceived vanity project, in which Spacey—as writer, director and star— takes an amazing showbiz story and kills it dead. The casting of Spacey, the movie's reason for being, is also its central flaw. He's wrong for the role in every possible way...It's a project that didn't call for a green light but rather an intervention."[379]

While few reviewers were as explicit as LaSalle, the consensus among many was that the quadruply-credited Kevin had just taken on too much responsibility for the project—"the result is, you're left feeling like you've OD-ed on Spacey,"[380] as Shebah Ronay put it in *The News of the World*. He was even ridiculed at the Toronto premiere of the film for arriving with what appeared to be black spray-paint applied to the back of his head to cover his thinning hair.

Spacey (who had to endure the nickname "Spraycey" in the tabloids for several months afterwards) later explained to an interviewer that "It's not a spray...At every single premiere or television appearance that I have done in the last six years I have always put a little make-up on the back of my head for the simple purpose of not letting the television lights see the beach-front property. My hair has been going since I was in my twenties."[381] This was an inheritance from his mother Kathleen, who wore a succession of wigs in public from her thirties onward: in contrast, father Geoff retained a full, thick head of hair to the end of his life.

Kevin was also slated in the press by actor Jeffrey Meek, who claimed to have sold him several Darin-based scripts during *Beyond's* long development process. "[Spacey] bought my material and then acted like I didn't exist," Meek fumed. "I'm not saying I'm Rembrandt, but it's like someone buying a painting and then scratching the name off of it and putting their own there."[382] A Writer's Guild arbitration hearing gave a co-credit for the final filmed screenplay to Lewis Colick, who had first produced a Darin-themed draft script for Warner Brothers in 1987.

Colick was reluctant to accept this acknowledgement, stating that "stylistically, [*Beyond the Sea*] is not me. Kevin Spacey took Bobby Darin's life and kind of ran with it…"[383] Several other writers who had submitted Darin-based screenplays to Warner Brothers, including *Taxi Driver* scribe Paul Schrader, asked not to be credited on *Beyond the Sea*, feeling the film was "too far removed" from their original material.

Award committees seemed equally unenthusiastic about the biopic. The only major accolade Kevin received was a lone Golden Globe nomination for Best Actor in A Motion Picture Musical or Comedy (he lost to Jamie Foxx for *Ray*),[384] while *Chicago*, released two years ahead of *Beyond the Sea*, won more Oscars than *American Beauty*.

The film Spacey had struggled to make for so long, then, was not exactly the rousing tribute to Darin he had hoped for. A standalone compilation of Bobby's best-known songs might perhaps have been a better idea, since *Beyond the Sea's* accompanying soundtrack album received far more favourable write-ups than the movie itself. To promote the film, in December 2004 Kevin toured several U.S. cities with a 19-member band performing Darin numbers. Although these concerts were popular, the failure of *Beyond the Sea* at the box office suggests the attendees were not as keen to watch a celluloid Spacey-as-Darin as they were to see him in the flesh (a planned stage musical version has yet to be produced).[385]

More ill-advised ventures were to follow. One of Kevin's next films, *Edison*, the story of a cub reporter, Josh Pollack (Justin Timberlake), who attempts to infiltrate a den of corrupt undercover policemen, was so badly panned at the Toronto Film Festival that it did not even merit a U.S. cinema release, ending up on the dreaded "direct to video" shelf instead. Direly scripted[386] and insipidly acted, *Edison* (the title refers to the town in which the movie takes place) plays like a failed TV pilot.

Spacey's character, Special Investigator Levon Wallace, is a cheap Jack Vincennes knockoff. Seemingly happy to look the other way as the elite "First Response Assault & Tactical" squad make their shady deals, he finally sees the light after the nosey Josh and his girlfriend Willow (Piper Perabo) are beaten up by a gang of enraged F.R.A.T. boys. Spacey (along with another usually reliable actor, Morgan Freeman) gives a bland performance and is outclassed by both ex-boyband member Timberlake and his own freakishly quiffed hairpiece. Fortunately for Kevin, though, a whole new phase of his career was just beginning.

# Chapter Ten
# Spacey Vic-Torious

*"I really don't want to spend my life doing a movie, movie, and then a play here and there–this gives me a purpose..."*
–Kevin Spacey on his appointment as Old Vic theatrical director (2003)

*"Because I've done films, I'm a Hollywood movie star, it's just about glamour and luvviness and all that crap."*
–Kevin Spacey on his "prejudiced" portrayal by the British press (2005)[387]

The Old Vic: what a lady. A strong contender for the title of Britain's most famous theatre, not soon confused with the "Queen Vic" (though she almost became a themed pub herself in 1998), she was founded in 1818 as the Royal Coburg, briefly becoming The New Victoria and then the Royal Victoria Coffee and Music Hall–the word "theatre" having being dropped in the 1880s because of its "impure associations."

Already nicknamed "the Old Vic," the snappier name stuck and passed into history under the formidable Lilian Baylis, who took over management of the building in 1912 and staged several Shakespeare productions, leading to the formation of the famous Old Vic Company in 1929. The Company (then including John Gielgud) were forced to tour the provinces when bombing damaged the theatre during the Blitz, but it was re-opened in 1950 and they continued staging Shakespeare there until 1963, when the National Theatre–which moved to its own eponymous premises in 1976–was founded by Sir Laurence Olivier.

The Old Vic gained a new owner, Canadian businessman Ed Mirvish, in 1982. Mirvish restored her to her pre-war glory–the current façade is based on an 1830 engraving, the auditorium on the designs of 1871. By the late-1990s, however, the theatre was back on the market and narrowly escaped being turned into a lap-dancing club, pub or bingo hall when she was purchased by The Old Vic Theatre Trust 2000, a charitable association set up by impresario Sally Greene. One of the first productions in the newly liberated building was Eugene O'Neill's mammoth 1939 masterwork, *The Iceman Cometh*, which transferred from the nearby Almeida in June 1998 and featured a certain Kevin Spacey in the central role of garrulous preacher's son Theodore Hickman.[388]

First staged in 1946, *The Iceman Cometh* takes place in a rundown saloon-cum-boarding house, home to a shabby set of down-and-outs, bitter men who talk big and do little. Into the mix comes Hickey, the group's showman, a recent teetotaller who makes it his mission to force the others to put away their poisonous "pipe dreams" and face the truth of their empty lives—as he did, it turns out, by murdering his neglected wife and thus "setting her free."

Jason Robards, a favourite actor of Kevin's, had featured in a 1985 revival of *Iceman* at the Kennedy Center in Washington. Spacey, who was then appearing in *A Seagull* at the same venue, later recounted that he "would sneak into the presidential box...to watch the master, night after night. For a master Hickey he was. I must have seen a dozen performances."[389] In a 2005 interview with *Premiere*, Spacey listed his "idols" as Robards, Lemmon, Spencer Tracy, Henry Fonda, Jimmy Stewart and Al Pacino: the omission of Katharine Hepburn is surprising.[390]

Spacey's own performance in *Iceman* was his most celebrated theatrical appearance since *Lost in Yonkers* and won him the *Evening Standard*, London Critics Circle and Olivier Awards for Best Actor (he was the first American to receive the coveted Olivier), plus another Tony nomination when *Iceman* moved to Broadway in March 1999. At his insistence and out of respect for the other 23 actors in the play, Spacey got equal alphabetical billing, shared a communal dressing room and was paid union minimum ($1,135 a week during the Broadway run, £260 a week (about $430) for the London one), despite being a co-producer and devoting nearly two years of his time to the show.

Spacey's last theatrical performance prior to *Iceman* was in an off-Broadway production of Athol Fugard's anti-apartheid drama *Playland* in the summer of 1993, almost five years previously. His hiatus in films had enhanced rather than impaired his stagecraft, as John Peter of *The Sunday Times*–a Spacey enthusiast since 1986–observed in a contemporary review:

> "Kevin Spacey is a good decade too young for the role, too athletic and virile; but he brings with him a sense of barely concealed unease, of a hidden tension about to explode…It is a performance of great energy under iron control, and of a vibrant sensitivity under surveillance, almost imperceptible but quite unerring, of a deeply theatrical intelligence. Spacey is a film star, but he began his career as a stage actor, and it shows."[391]

Alastair Macaulay of *The Financial Times* added: "To watch him without the intervention of the camera is a privilege; one can really observe–indeed, breathe in–the way he lights up the nervous system of his character from within."[392] *Iceman* was directed by Howard Davies, who had championed Spacey as Alan Rickman's replacement in *Les Liaisons Dangereuses* over a decade before–the memory of Kevin's superlative audition had stuck with him to such an extent that Spacey was the first person he thought of for the leading part. "We thought it was very unlikely we'd actually get him because of his busy film schedule," Davies later said, "but we tried. That very day we put in a call to his personal manager, and two weeks later we got Kevin's answer: yes."[393]

"What he's doing is what we all do in our lives," Davies commented on Spacey's highly lauded role. "We conduct ourselves on several levels. What Kevin manages to do with his acting is hint at all these other layers–the darker aspects, the secrets, the disappointments, the ironic humor. And that hinting is very, very attractive."[394] Kevin's portrayal of Hickey even inspired artist Nick Barnes (of the group Blind Summit) to model one of the tragic drunks in his adult puppet show *Low Life* on him.

On 4th February 2003, the front page of *The Times* announced: "Kevin Spacey to run the Old Vic." At a press conference to confirm the appointment the following day the actor stated that he would appear in "at least two productions a season," as well as directing, and promised to bring both fellow Hollywood stars and new talent into the theatre. Spacey enthused: "To have grown up to act on the stage itself was a dream come true. To find myself in the role of director of the Old Vic is beyond my wildest imaginings."

Spacey also related the fabricated story of his "frequent" trips to London as a tot. "My parents took theatre trips from America to London starting when I was around seven years old. I remember seeing Shakespeare and other productions on the Old Vic stage. Some of my earliest memories of the theatre experience itself surround these family trips to England," he blithely told the watching millions. While *The Times* had stated "it is thought that Spacey might also use the conference to end the speculation in the media about his sexuality,"[395] unsurprisingly, this was one opportunity Kevin declined.

The reaction from the hoi polloi was initially one of bemusement. Kevin Spacey, the American film bloke? Whilst the theatre had had celebrity artistic directors before–notably, of course, Olivier[396]–at least they'd had the good sense to be British. But Spacey, who had joined The Old Vic Theatre Trust's board back in 1998, seemed genuinely committed to the theatre's cause, as can be seen in his almost messianic account of how he came to accept the post:

> "It's just about timing. I was doing *The Iceman Cometh* at the Old Vic…I fell in love with the place–the building, the feeling you have there. I was asked to be on the committee to help find an artistic director. And the truth was I didn't feel like I knew enough about its history. We gathered about 40 people to have a discussion about what it was about and our mission, and everyone agreed it was at its best when it was an actor's theater. [After] I left there that night, I couldn't sleep. So I got into a cab, I went to the Old Vic, and it was raining. I was standing in front of it, and I realized, What are you doing? You want a change, you want something outside your career, and you want something lasting. So I threw my hat in the ring."[397]

Spacey had first agreed to take on the artistic directorship of the Old Vic shortly after *American Beauty's* London premiere in November 1999, but managed to keep the decision secret for over three years. "Two years from now I will be in a place where I could dedicate myself to a lot more theatre,"[398] he told a reporter in February 2002, one of several "hints" he dropped to the media about his upcoming new job around this time. Clearly this was no publicity stunt. At last, the ultimate actor's actor truly "owned the stage."

Spacey's management plans seem to have begun early. "The dream of running a theatre for me started when I was 13," he said in 2006. "I grew up in the San Fernando Valley and my best friend [Val Kilmer] lived on a ranch that was built by Roy Rogers, the old cowboy star. We dreamed of building a theatre there. We were going to do Shakespeare and new plays and we were going to broaden the world, challenge ourselves. I still have the napkins where we drew up the designs of the amphitheatre."[399] He also revealed that he contributes his yearly £100,000 salary to the Old Vic's coffers.

Spacey has often spoken of his preference for stagecraft over filmcraft, telling one interviewer in 2002 that "Usually, when I've managed to get close to something it's been in the theatre, because it just seems more tangible, somehow. It hasn't disappeared off in a can somewhere, and then months go by and I see it and go 'Oh, that's what they've ended up doing.' You're simply not a part of the decision-making about what a movie's going to end up being."[400]

In early 2000 Spacey said: "Every emotional, personal and artistic important experience for me happens in the theatre. Everything I do on stage is good for film acting. I could never have played Lester [in *American Beauty*] without my experience in *The Iceman Cometh*. I would never have touched the spirit of this role or played it with the empathy I needed. I can't imagine my work anymore without having to go through a character, like you do on stage every night."[401] He put it even more simply in a conversation with Michael Colgan, director of London's Gate Theatre. As Colgan related: "I said to Kevin Spacey, 'it's great that you do these plays in between the films.' 'Michael,' he said, 'I do the films in between the plays.'"[402]

"One day I'll fall over on the stage," Spacey joked in another 2000 interview. "That's how I'll go."[403] Kevin–a popular figure at theatrical galas since *Iceman*–was soon taken to the heart of the "Establishment," even donning a kitsch pink Seventies-style outfit to co-host a £1000-a-head fundraising event with his friend–and Old Vic chairman–Elton John shortly after his Old Vic appointment was made public. The party to celebrate his new job drew a host of luminaries including Sir Richard Branson, Lord Attenborough and Peter Mandelson.[404] The ardent Anglophile was an honorary Brit already. John Graham Spacey would have been proud.

So would mother Kathleen, but for the first time in Kevin's life, she was unable to share in his success. Since Geoff's death, Kathleen, finally freed of her husband's stifling influence, had used the remainder of her lottery winnings to travel widely across the U.S. and Europe, visiting friends and relatives and meeting new acquaintances (including, in her capacity as a member of the Charles Dickens Fellowship, the author's great-grandson, Cedric).[405]

Kathleen accompanied her son to many movie premieres and award ceremonies, even making a cameo appearance in *Midnight in the Garden of Good and Evil* as a party guest,[406] and was also by his side–along with Kevin's old drama teacher, Robert Carrelli–when he received his star on the Hollywood Walk of Fame in October 1999. In March 2002, though, she suffered a seizure on the way to a train station in Seattle and was later diagnosed with a brain tumour. Spacey moved his mother to a leased apartment in Los Angeles, where radiation treatment was attempted,[407] but the tumour eventually proved inoperable.

Kathleen Knutson Fowler died on 19th March 2003, her daughter Julie's fifty-second birthday, six weeks after Spacey's new role at the Old Vic was announced. Her obituary notice, like her husband's, was posted in *Variety*, which noted in a by-line that she was "Mother of Kevin Spacey, poet, musician."[408] While Geoff Fowler had been interred in a burial plot in Georgia, Kathleen–who had moved from the oversized Lawrenceville property to a small condo in Gig Harbor, Washington State, in late 2000– chose to be cremated after death rather than laid to rest beside her husband.

Kathleen's ashes were divided among her three children and sealed in pewter containers shaped like starfish, embossed with a gold panel with her favourite saying: "Everything will be fine."[409] A memorial plaque (which, in yet another family ambiguity, shows Kathleen's year of birth as 1932 rather than 1931, thus raising the possibility that she added a year to her age in her youth to facilitate her early marriage) is now on display in the Forest Lawn Memorial Park in the Hollywood Hills. It reads: "KATHLEEN: A TRUE FRIEND TO ALL. SHE LOVED BOOKS, VANILLA LATTES, KATHYSPEAK AND "WHATEVER"–YOUR DEVOTED AND LOVING FAMILY AND FRIENDS."

Kevin was criticised by certain sectors of the Press for not immediately discussing the death of the woman who had been his only constant public companion for the previous decade; to a man as private as Spacey, this must have seemed a grossly insensitive charge. In an attempt to avoid publicity, he had had Kathleen's funeral service conducted under a false name–Ruby Stevens, the birth name of actress Barbara Stanwyck–and was listed in the related newspaper notices as a "guest" rather than a son of the deceased.[410] The following year, however, he was effusive in his tribute to her final days:

> "It's not easy to say this, but during that time we had a remarkable experience. You see, even though I was the one trying to help, she was the one helping me, by setting the tone. The doctors said there would be a period of denial, and then acceptance. But she skipped the denial and went right to acceptance. My mother had one of the great senses of humor that I have ever known, and she kept us laughing right to the end. It was an incredibly beautiful time, to be able to spend endless hours and hours together…"[411]

Kevin had noted in 2001 that "My mother and I have a very malicious sense of humour. It's very wry and dry," evidenced by her comments at the funeral home in 1992 after her youngest son assured her that the recently-deceased Geoff made a handsome corpse: "These people [other mourners] are going to think that we killed him for insurance money because we were laughing at his funeral." Upon realising that Geoff's Scottish pocket watch had stopped at the exact time of his death, Kathleen quipped: "Well, when your time is up, your time is up!"[412]

Kathleen never got to see *Beyond the Sea*, Kevin's Bobby Darin biopic, but she is an integral part of the film's history. As David Evanier noted:

"There's the connection with his mother. Bobby's mother's[413] belief in him sent him soaring. Kevin's mother wanted him to make this film. Kevin sees the film as an act of devotion to his mother."[414]

"I think the movie is about mothers and sons," Spacey concurred. "I made the movie for all mothers, but especially for my mother…I'm glad she passed knowing this was the movie I was going to make."[415] He had earlier expressed similar sentiments in an interview with *The Observer*: "It's the movie my mother wanted me to do more than any movie I've ever done. It's my personal statement."[416]

During his concert tour to promote the film, Spacey performed at Bimbo's 365 Club in San Francisco on Kathleen's birthday and regaled the audience (which included his sister Julie) with stories of how he had first "been introduced" to Darin through his mom: he dedicated the song "Once Upon A Time" to her the following night. A credit at *Beyond's* end simply reads: "for Mother." Kathleen is commemorated at the Old Vic, too. A seat in the stalls bears a plaque to her memory.

Following his mother's death, the "older woman" Kevin was most likely to escort to premieres was actress Judi Dench, who had made her professional debut with the Old Vic Company in 1957. Three years Kathleen's junior, Dench became friendly with Spacey when appearing across the street from *Iceman* in the play *Amy's View* on Broadway in 1999, later co-starring as his aunt in *The Shipping News*. "Working with her was like being in the desert and finding a well of the most delicious water that you could possibly hope to find…"[417] he stated in 2001.

Judi's husband, actor Michael Williams, who had been suffering from lung cancer, passed away during pre-production of the film. In March 2002, during an appearance on Michael Parkinson's chat show, she revealed that Kevin had been instrumental in keeping her spirits up in the months following her bereavement, organising games of pool and Ping-Pong at their hotel and teaching her how to ride his electric scooter during a weekend break in Central Park. Spacey, who appeared on the show with her, took the opportunity to showcase the dancing skills he had honed during his youthful musical theatre days, coaxing the chary Parkinson into an impromptu tap routine.

When Dench received a Special Award from the Laurence Olivier Society in February 2004 for her "outstanding contribution to British theatre" she was moved to tears after Spacey serenaded her with the George Gershwin classic "I've Got A Crush On You" during the ceremony. Kevin praised "a woman of enormous grace and style and friendship and conviction whose spirit and integrity are as infectious as her laugh." Referring back to his song, he added: "There is no one like her and there never will be anyone like her. She is the one we have all had a crush on for a very long time." But for the last sentence, he could have been talking about Kathleen.

When asked by one interviewer if he minded if she "started a rumour that you're in love with Judi Dench?" Spacey chuckled: "That wouldn't be a rumour. I've said that publicly. She's naughty, she cheats at ping-pong, she's a giggler–I love to make her giggle."[418] Judi's all-subsuming acting style is somewhat similar to Kevin's, as a 1998 *New York Times* article that discussed the stage performances of Spacey, Dench and comic Martin Short noted:

> "None of this trio gives off the megawatt glamour or Personality with a capital P usually associated with stars. They are all, by self-definition, chameleons, and anyone who knows their work has marveled at the different colorings they seem to assume so reflexively. They have technique to spare, for sure, but they are also propelled by something far more potent: the fierce, fluid will to become someone else."[419]

Fans eager to see the Oscar-winning star himself strut his stuff on the London stage again were in for a long wait. Due to Kevin's prior filming commitments (principally *Beyond the Sea*), the official press conference to announce the new season's programme was not held until over a year after his appointment and was overshadowed by a mysterious incident in Geraldine Mary Harmsworth Park, close to the theatre, a few days beforehand.

At approximately 4.30 am on 17th April 2004, Kevin staggered into Kennington Police Station, blood dripping from a wound in his head, and reported to the officer in charge that he had been mugged while taking his dog, Mini, for a late-night defecation. Later that day, however, Spacey withdrew the allegation, claiming instead that a young man had conned him out of his mobile phone,[420] and he'd received a bump on the head when he tripped over Mini's lead whilst pursuing the alleged thief.

Kevin subsequently gave a detailed account of the "mugging" on BBC Radio 4's *Today Programme:*

> "What actually happened is, I fell for a con. And I was, I think, incredibly embarrassed by it. Some sob story about somebody needing to call their mother and could they use my phone. It was such a good con, that I actually dialled the number myself and when somebody answered I then finally handed [over] my phone. And this kid took off and I was so upset I ran after him. It was late in the morning and I was walking my dog, it was about 4 am, and I tripped up over my dog, and I ended up falling on to the street and hitting myself in the head.
>
> And now I'm bleeding relatively profusely, I'm extremely upset, I feel like the biggest fool that has ever lived. I march over to the police station and I say I got mugged. And I'm thinking they are going to run out and find this kid a block later. Of course they take me to the hospital, and they were very kind."[421]

It was a bizarre tale, especially given that the area is known to be a popular cottaging site for gay men. As one local postman told *The Sun*: "I go past the park most mornings very early and often see a few dodgy looking characters hanging around the bushes and they don't seem to be looking at the flowers…"[422] The tabloid later published a poetic variation of "The Teddy Bears' Picnic" (entitled "The Seedy, Bare Picnic") in Kevin's "honour."

Tom Junod, who had so controversially "outed" Spacey seven years earlier in *Esquire*, noted of the incident: "What happened leaves me surprised because Kevin is the most studied, controlled person I have ever come across. He doesn't raise an eyebrow without knowing he is raising that eyebrow. I've never known him not to be in control of events, and his image."[423] The services of Spacey's Beverly Hills attorney, Doug

Stone, were swiftly employed to discourage the more salacious Fleet Street newspapers from suggesting that he had visited the park with an ulterior motive in mind.

At the press conference to promote his first production, *Cloaca*–filled with tabloid reporters uncharacteristically showing a strong interest in culture–a smirking Spacey joked that "I'd like to put to rest a rumour that has been spreading about town for the past few days which I think is entirely unfair. That is"–dramatic pause–"that David Beckham offered to donate 100,000 pounds to The Old Vic if I would take him off the front pages for a few days" (Beckham, the British football star, was then the subject of intense media gossip accusing him of cheating on his Spice Girl wife Victoria with bisexual pin-up Rebecca Loos).

"Just to be sure, my plan is to text David myself–if someone will let me borrow their mobile, because I seem to have misplaced mine," Spacey added. Attempting to put the topic to rest, he concluded, "I think I just heard the sound of a very large elephant leaving the theatre."

During the conference, Spacey appeared distinctly ill at ease. Nevertheless, many members of the public took his comments at face value and assumed the whole mugging incident to have been a hoax. Kevin could do little to prevent the papers calling in another source, however. *The Mail on Sunday* approached elder brother Randy for feedback and it was then that the allegations about Geoff's abusive character and Nazi connections first surfaced.

In the immediate aftermath of the *Mail* story, the subject was occasionally raised by a journalist or two.[424] Met with a curt "no comment" by Spacey–surely the only sensible public response–the charges against his father gradually faded from the collective media mind and it can perhaps be assumed that anyone hoping for an interview with Geoff's youngest son these days is advised not to mention the article.

While the new Artistic Director had no problems winning over London's glitterati, theatre critics proved rather harder to sway. Masculine mid-life crisis drama *Cloaca*–by little-known Dutch writer Maria Goos, the word translates from Latin as "sewer"–which Spacey directed, seemed a strange choice with which to open the new season and was predictably condemned as a "stinker."[425]

Audiences, however, many eager to catch a glimpse of Kevin at the stage door, flocked to the production and were usually rewarded with an autograph and a chance to have their photo taken with their hero.[426] While ticket sales had fallen somewhat by the time *Cloaca* ended its run in early December, the theatre generally played to three-thirds capacity in September and October, with advance ticket sales topping £500,000: not a bad record by West End standards.

The majority of plays directly involving Spacey made money, even when reviews were savage. In the first year, he appeared in both yuppie satire *National Anthems*–as deluded firefighter Ben Cook, a role he had first enacted at Connecticut's Long Wharf Theater in 1988[427]–and Thirties romcom *The Philadelphia Story*, critically unlauded but playing to a full house.

"No one could accuse Spacey of being blessed with [Cary] Grant's dark good looks–there is always something faintly reptilian about him–but he is one of those actors you simply can't take your eyes off,"[428] a somewhat snarky Charles Spencer noted in a rare complimentary review of *The Philadelphia Story* in *The Telegraph*. Another early success was the Christmas pantomime *Aladdin*, featuring Sir Ian McKellen as Widow Twankey, a role he reprised the following year (it had long been an ambition of the acclaimed theatrical knight to play a panto dame, apparently).

The first Spacey play to really find favour with reviewers was his U.K. Shakespearean debut, *Richard II*. Opening Kevin's second season in October 2005 and directed by the venerable Sir Trevor Nunn, the new *Richard* was an innovative and powerful production in which Spacey (whose English accent had improved considerably since his *See No Evil* days)[429] played the titular role in modern dress, ubiquitous mobile phone in hand.

The touch of cold arrogance which had worked against Kevin in so many of his post-*Beauty* film parts was an asset here, as Victoria Segal of *The Sunday Times* noted:

> "Spacey is not normally an actor who offers intimacy: he has an oddly shuttered quality, a sense of tight control that can border

on the glib. Like an emotional fruit machine, he makes the right noises and flashes the right lights, but is reluctant to pay out. Here, however, he comes close to hitting the jackpot with a Richard who is commanding and charismatic, but far from regal, a man given to intemperate rages, bitchy asides, mocking sighs...

Spacey is still not an easy actor to love, yet, here, the shadow of self-regard that sometimes clouds his performances is perfect shading for this flawed and fragile king. It's a canny choice of role–complex, ambiguous and ultimately touched with grace. If his future choices are as astute, his story at the Old Vic has at last found the promise of a happy ending."[430]

*Richard II* won two awards (including Best Actor) at the Theatregoers' Choice ceremony, chosen by public vote, and Kevin received the John and Wendy Trewin prize for best Shakespearean performance at the 2005 Critics Circle Theatre Awards. The following year, however, he suffered his first bona fide disaster after inviting veteran director Robert Altman (who had not worked on the stage for over twenty years) to the Old Vic to supervise the British premiere of the late Arthur Miller's *Resurrection Blues*.

Miller's play, a satirical political drama based around the planned execution of a mysterious Christ-like prisoner in an unnamed Latin American country, had first been performed in the U.S. in 2002. The Old Vic's version had reasonable advance bookings on the strength of the playwright, director, and well-known stars such as Matthew Modine, Neve Campbell and James Fox, but this time later attendance was poor, with the auditorium often less than half-full despite some tickets being offered on a "buy one, get one free" basis.

Ineptly staged, poorly acted, and incoherently scripted–Miller was still working on revisions when he died–the production proved an embarrassment for all concerned and ended its run (in April 2006) a week earlier than planned after ticket sales failed to improve. American actress Jane Adams had already quit, storming off the stage in the middle of a matinee performance after a fight with Modine.

To make matters worse, there were no other shows scheduled until September, meaning that the Old Vic would effectively be left empty for five months. Producer Tom Kinninmont offered to stage the play *Jeffrey Bernard Is Unwell*, with Tom Conti, over the summer, but attempts to negotiate with Spacey collapsed after two weeks, apparently due to the excessive costs of keeping the theatre's bar open.

Spacey himself refused to accept any liability for the *Resurrection* debacle, laying it squarely at the feet of the performers—whom he had helped to cast. "We worked hard to get the play to a point where it could be appreciated," he told *The Guardian's* Michael Billington. "Now, unfortunately, opening night came and those actors got hit by a set of nerves the like of which I've never seen."[431]

This attitude, unsurprisingly, did not improve his popularity in journalistic circles. *The Evening Standard's* theatre critic, Nicholas de Jongh, was particularly scathing, asking: "Is it time for Kevin Spacey to hand over his crown? The Old Vic's latest show is a flop...If the theatre goes dark, its artistic director should resign...he has landed his theatre in a genuine, glittering crisis for which he must take responsibility...He simply is not competent to be running the Old Vic."[432]

Kevin blamed the media for using his celebrity as a weapon, claiming he was "being put under a bigger microscope" than any other new artistic director would be. "Things also happen here that happen at every theatre in this country. But because my name can be placed in a headline, the press rake over everything since I arrived. And my only question is—are we being judged on a level playing field? But I'm not going to get into a debate with the press I can't win."[433]

He also re-iterated his pledge to see out his contract: "This is a 10-year commitment. I am now more determined than ever."[434] The public were firmly behind Kevin: a mid-2005 survey by theatre website www.whatsonstage.com found that 80% of respondents believed the actor had done well in his first year, and 68% felt the media had been "unfair."

True to his word, come September, Spacey bounced back in blazing form with a starring role in Eugene O'Neill's last completed play, *A Moon for the Misbegotten*, a sequel of sorts to *Long Day's Journey Into Night*. He was directed once again by Howard Davies and played an older, more dissolute version of Jamie Tyrone from the earlier work.

Now in his early forties, Jamie is a truly wretched figure, spitting insults at the deceased James Sr.–"lousy tightwad bastard"[435]–and consumed with guilt over having fallen prey to "the old booze yen"[436] when his sick mother lapsed into a coma after developing a brain tumour. "I went crazy," says Jamie to would-be lover Josie (played by Eve Best), as his self-loathing gradually destroys their burgeoning relationship. "Couldn't face losing her."[437]

The loss of his own mother in similar circumstances must have made it difficult for Kevin to take the part, but he didn't disappoint, the critical plaudits for his performance equalling his *Iceman* and *American Beauty* acclaim. "After a summer of darkness, and a string of famous upsets, Kevin Spacey's theatre has delivered an hour that's worth crossing the country for: a duet between Spacey and Eve Best unmatched for intensity elsewhere in the London theatre,"[438] raved Susannah Clapp in *The Observer*.

"Spacey has certainly had his ups and downs as the Old Vic's artistic director," added Christopher Hart of *The Sunday Times*, "but this is an almost unqualified triumph. By the end of the evening, the actors look much like we feel: wrung out emotionally, exhausted but triumphant."[439]

*Moon* reinforced Spacey's reputation as one of the best "O'Neillian" actors around and won him his second consecutive Theatregoers' Choice Award for Best Actor. It successfully transferred to the Brooks Atkinson Theater–the site of both his Broadway debut in *Ghosts* and his Tony nominated tour-de-force in *The Iceman Cometh*–in March 2007.

The following year Kevin was again sublime in the David Mamet-penned Hollywood satire *Speed-the-Plow*, his cynical producer Charlie Fox–"Life in the movie business is like the beginning of a new love affair: it's full of surprises, and you're constantly getting fucked"[440]–recalling überexec Buddy Ackerman in *Swimming With Sharks*. In *The New York Times*, an impressed Matt Wolf reflected:

> "In the litany of great theatrical double-acts in London, there's a reasonably familiar roll call: Sirs John Gielgud and Ralph Richardson, say, or, more recently, Dames Maggie Smith and Judi Dench. Now comes a near-peerless pairing that talks with an

American accent: Jeff Goldblum and Kevin Spacey, who, separately and together, achieve what a different sector of American society might refer to as liftoff in their partnership on the Old Vic stage… [the] final passages of the play restore Spacey to the sense of a talent coming dizzyingly unleashed that was first evident on the West End stage when he appeared in 1986 in *Long Day's Journey Into Night…*"[441]

A month earlier, Spacey was the subject of an–in the words of one critic–"extraordinarily sycophantic"[442] edition of ITV's *South Bank Show* which profiled his Old Vic achievements. Faced with Kevin's potent blend of menace and charm, even veteran host Melvyn Bragg got giggly.

In June 2008, Kevin Spacey was appointed as Cameron Mackintosh Visiting Professor of Contemporary Theatre at St. Catherine's College, Oxford, succeeding RSC actor Patrick Stewart in the post. Spacey seemed genuinely thrilled with yet another nod from the British theatrical elite: "It really is an honour for me to have been invited to follow such illustrious names and take up this role at Oxford…I relish the challenge ahead and am excited for term to begin."[443]

Five months later, Kevin received a special prize from *The Evening Standard* Theatre Award committee for "bringing new life to the Old Vic" (he was also nominated for Best Actor for *Speed-the-Plow*). On the judging panel: one Nicholas de Jongh. "In my 17 years [here] I cannot recall many occasions when there was a more exciting and diverse collection of candidates in most of the categories…London theatre now offers tremendous choice for theatre-goers,"[444] the now-converted Spacey-phile said. The critics were also impressed by Spacey's decision to present several productions in the 2008/09 season "in the round," moving the action to the centre of the auditorium by temporarily removing some of the stall seats and the chandelier.

More commendations followed. In April 2009, Kevin received the prestigious Monte Cristo Award from the Eugene O'Neill Theater Center in recognition of "his distinguished accomplishments and contributions to the American and international theater community."[445] He pulled off a major coup when he enticed virtuoso pal Sam Mendes back to the stage to direct Chekhov's *The Cherry Orchard* and Shakespeare's *The Winter's Tale* as part of the Bridge Project, an Anglo-American venture which involves a renowned international cast performing two selected plays at the Brooklyn Academy of Music and various venues across the globe before transferring to the Old Vic.

"We're starting to see that we are doing what I set out to try and do, which is to create the first transatlantic theatre company…it's exciting to go to other countries and give them opportunities to see an English language play they would never normally see unless they travelled to England or New York. To make an argument and a case for living theatre in as many places as we can is an extremely exciting prospect,"[446] Kevin enthused in a *Daily Telegraph* interview.

While claiming that "the theatre remains my primary allegiance," Spacey has also managed to fit several film roles into his schedule during his tenure at the Old Vic. He upset some theatregoers when he took seven weeks out from *The Philadelphia Story* to film the role of arch villain Lex Luthor in Bryan Singer's *Superman Returns*. "Ever since *The Usual Suspects*, [Kevin and I] had been looking for something to do together and he is extremely perfect for the role. He has just the right blend of humour and cynicism and, of course, he is simply a brilliant actor,"[447] Singer stated.

A spokeswoman for the theatre denied that there had been any attempt to "mask" the fact that Spacey was not due to appear in all the shows, but this did not placate many of the ticket-buyers who complained of "blatant misrepresentation."[448] ("I'm sure it'll command a nice fee, but it does send out a pretty strange message about his priorities…"[449] a less discreet Old Vic source admitted).

During the *Iceman* run in 1998, Spacey was unexpectedly called back to Los Angeles on 22nd July to attend the premiere of his film *The Negotiator*. Unwilling to disappoint those who had booked tickets for the theatrical performance he subsequently missed, Spacey agreed to an extra Sunday matinee on 26th July, the afternoon not just of his day off, but of his 39th birthday: this incident makes the *Superman* scheduling snafu seem all the more ill-judged. At least one critic saw it as symptomatic of a greater malaise:

"There's a new spirit about at the Old Vic, which is at odds not only with its distinguished history as the home of Laurence Olivier's National Theatre company, but also at odds with the spirit of theatre generally...Of course, it is entitled to play down the fact a star is leaving a production, even when it knows full well that a percentage of ticket buyers has paid out purely to see that star...The building is smarter; the glamorous atmosphere can be attractive. But some aspects of public performance should not change. Theatres should play fair with their audiences, and not allow them to buy tickets under a false assumption."[450]

Spacey promptly wrote a "long, firm but very courteous letter" to the writer of this article, stating that "everything possible" was done to warn ticket buyers of his absence from the show.[451] He clearly took the criticism to heart, however. Not wanting to disappoint his public further, he has since taken steps to ensure that his film and stage timetables do not overlap.

Now back in the character parts that he inhabits so well, Spacey's lively reinterpretation of classic comic strip bad guy Luthor–"Gods are the selfish beings who fly around in little red capes and don't share their power with mankind!" even prompted one reviewer to remark: "Spacey's cracking performance puts paid to the whisperings of mean-minded types in this country who claim he's only doing London theatre because his movie career is washed up. It's not."[452]

"So much better at bitching than caring and sharing, [Spacey is] a delight here," said another, "camping up his arch-baddie role, and investing it with a creepy, near-gerontophile sexuality that makes a far scarier Lex than Gene Hackman's straight-up thug rendering back in 1978."[453] Both Kevin's performance and natty suits in *Superman Returns* were inspired by a real-life baddie: Kenneth L. Lay, the dandyish former chief of disgraced U.S. energy giant Enron.

Kevin created another memorable villain in devious MIT tutor Micky Rosa, a much more credible Prof than David Gale, for sharp Vegas heist tale *21*. While he originally signed on to the project as producer only, the part had been written with him in mind (as was the case with *The Usual Suspects*) and he soon accepted an offer to star in the film as well. Spacey also scored a notable success with *Recount*, a 2008 TV film about the controversial 2000 "hanging chad" Florida election battle that eventually decided the U.S. Presidency in favour of George W. Bush.

Spacey portrayed his opponent Al Gore's former Chief of Staff Ron Klain (who knows Spacey socially) as well as–through Trigger Street–producing the film, which won a raft of awards including the Emmy for Best Made-For-Television Movie. Kevin's powerful performance (his choked "I just–I just couldn't get 'em counted" as the tenacious Klain is forced to concede defeat to the Republicans is the film's most affecting moment by far) saw him nominated for acting Emmy, Golden Globe and SAG awards: quite an impressive trio.

# Epilogue
# The Future's Spacey

*"Most actors aren't quite as mysterious as they seem once you see them up close."*
–Kevin Spacey (2004)[454]

*"Once you whet the public's appetite for the truth, the sky's the limit…"*
–Sid Hudgens, *L.A. Confidential* (1997)

Kevin Spacey reached his half-century on 26th July 2009, having garnered an impressive haul of trophies over the previous twenty years: one Tony, two Oscars, a BAFTA and countless other awards and nominations for his work on both stage and screen. His C.V. includes roles in such classic films as *Working Girl, Glengarry Glen Ross, Se7en, L.A. Confidential, American Beauty* and the superlative *Usual Suspects*, perhaps the greatest heist movie ever made.[455] One of the best-connected men in London, his close friends include a Prince, two Prime Ministers and a former U.S. President.

There is little sign of the sulky Spacey persona in interviews now. Recent questioners have reported meeting only the congenial, laid-back Kevin[456]–his reticent side rarely gets a look-in these days. He's an enthusiastic user of the online mini-blog Twitter (with a million-plus "followers" by the end of August 2009) who responds patiently to many of the countless fan "tweets" he receives, placing himself on the public arena more willingly than he has for years. His regular, affable updates–"Hope you all had a good day. Peace out"[457]–are testament to a more relaxed Spacey than the Kevin of 2001, struggling to find a worthy post-*Beauty* follow-up and producing only dross.

Halfway through his ten-year Old Vic contract, the man with a self-professed horror of "stagnation" seems to have finally hit on a winning formula. While the first few plays staged at the theatre under his tenure were panned, more recent productions–*A Moon for the Misbegotten*, *The Entertainer*, *All About My Mother*, *Speed-the-Plow*, *The Norman Conquests*, *Dancing at Lughnasa*–have done well both critically and commercially (creaky political drama *Complicit*, staged in January and February 2009, was the only dud).

The run of successes looks set to continue in 2010, when Sam Mendes will return to the famous stage to direct Shakespeare's *The Tempest* and *As You Like It* under Year Two of the innovative Bridge Project. The pressure to turn out a constant stream of work on celluloid is off and Kevin now only has to "go Hollywood" when the right script comes along. "My life is better," the self-confessed "obsessive" worker said simply in mid-2006. "I did not like the hot spot of being in the heat of it all. And quite frankly, it's been very valuable to take a little shine off my career. It's been really good, because I live a better life."[458]

It seems somehow symbolic that as Kevin celebrated his 50th birthday in New Orleans, where he was filming his new movie *Father of Invention*, a special gala was held at the Old Vic: the New Voices 24 Hour Plays, in which a company of fifty 18-25 year olds created and produced seven new plays in just 24 hours. "Raw talent, brazen ambition and sheer determination will result in an evening that is tipped to be the fastest-paced theatrical experience of the year,"[459] enthused the Old Vic press blurb.

Kevin must have been sorry to miss the gala, but he was there in spirit. He was instrumental in setting up the New Voices Club, a professional development programme for young actors, directors, writers and producers, which has a membership of 3,000 and creates 50 new productions annually. The Club has become so successful–an astonishing fifty-four of the plays staged at the 2007 Edinburgh Festival began life under the programme–that a companion project, the New Voices Network New York, has now been launched in the U.S.

Spacey has also introduced several initiatives to encourage young people into the theatre, including drama workshops, school tours and cut-price seats for the under-25s, a policy he had previously championed during the *Iceman* run to enable hard-up students to see the play. "Some of my favourite days are the workshop days when there are around 1,000 kids running around, charging through the place and developing and learning how to collaborate. I just believe in it because I was a beneficiary of it when I was a kid," he said in 2006, recalling his first teenage encounter with Jack Lemmon.

"The confidence that this gives a person—I just know that you can have a lot to do with a kid's self-confidence, with their character building. The truth is that people can do really remarkable things when they start to think they can accomplish stuff and when they discover that, as far as I'm concerned, they've discovered the first secret of success...It's not that I have great pearls of wisdom but we do have a great education programme."[460] Kevin's "elevator" must be pretty full by now, but he's still sending it back down...

Maybe Kevin Spacey is learning how to be himself at last.

Here's to the next 50 years!

# The Beautiful People

The "beautiful people"–who usually are not,
But because of their money–a phrase they have bought.

With neurotic, psychotic-type lives they are fraught;
For all of their millions, peace of mind they have not.

They're jetting all over from Singapore to Rome,
Still convinced that their money makes anywhere home.

A sample of misery, none better you'll find.
To real happiness they are ever so blind.

The genuinely beautiful people you meet
Have a character pure and a heart oh so sweet.

They have learned how to live with the tides of defeat,
And with life, show a willingness, still to compete.

They are gentle and kind, and a goodness display
To help out a dear friend, will go out of their way.

They have something the "monied" can rarely afford,
Time and conscience to be in atune with the Lord.

by Kathleen Knutson Fowler[461]

# Bibliography

Ball, Alan. *American Beauty*. London: FilmFour Books, 1999.

Beane, Douglas Carter. *The Little Dog Laughed*. New York: Dramatists Play Service Inc, 2007.

Berendt, John. *Midnight in the Garden of Good and Evil*. London: Sceptre, 2009.

Chekhov, Anton (translated and introduced by David Magarshack). *Four Plays: The Seagull, Uncle Vanya, The Three Sisters, The Cherry Orchard*. London: George Allen & Unwin Ltd, 1970.

Dargis, Manohla. *BFI Modern Classics: L.A. Confidential*. London: BFI Publishing, 2003.

Dyer, Richard. *BFI Modern Classics: Seven*. London: BFI Publishing, 1999.

Editors of Time Magazine. *Time Almanac 2009*. New York: Time Publishers, 2008.

Ehrenstein, David. *Open Secret: Gay Hollywood 1928-2000*. New York: HarperCollins, 2000.

Ellroy, James. *The Dudley Smith Trio: The Big Nowhere, L.A. Confidential, White Jazz*. London: Arrow Books, 1999.

Evanier, David. *Roman Candle: The Life of Bobby Darin*. Emmaus: Rodale, 2004.

Ewing, Jack. *Spacey's Brother: Out of the Closet. The Authorized Biography of Randy B. Fowler*. Unpublished manuscript, 2005.

Fugard, Athol. *Playland*. London: Faber and Faber Limited, 1993.

Fuller, Nick. *Call Me Bud: Jack Lemmon On Film*. Sandy: Authors OnLine Ltd, 2008.

Grant, Richard E. *With Nails: The film diaries of Richard E. Grant*. London: Picador, 1997.

Green, Jonathon. *Cassell's Dictionary of Slang*. London: Cassell & Co., 2002.

Hadleigh, Boze. *Celebrity Diss & Tell*. Kansas City: Andrews McMeel Publishing, 2005.

Hamilton, William. *Blessed, Life and Films of Val Kilmer*. Milton Keynes: CreateSpace, 2008.

Harper, Kenn (foreword by Kevin Spacey). *Give Me My Father's Body*. London: Profile Books Ltd, 2001.

Ibsen, Henrik (introduction by James McFarlane). *Four Major Plays: A Doll's House, Ghosts, Hedda Gabler, The Master Builder*. Oxford: Oxford University Press, 1992.

Larsen, Ernest. *BFI Modern Classics: The Usual Suspects*. London: BFI Publishing, 2002.

Lemmon, Chris (foreword by Kevin Spacey). *A Twist of Lemmon: A Tribute to My Father*. North Carolina: Algonquin Books of Chapel Hill, 2006.

McIntyre, Dennis. *National Anthems*. London: Faber and Faber Limited, 2005.

McQuarrie, Christopher. *The Usual Suspects*. London: Faber and Faber Limited, 2000.

Mamet, David. *Speed-the-Plow*. London: Methuen Books, 1994.

O'Neill, Eugene (introduction by Christine Dymkowski). *The Iceman Cometh*. London: Nick Hern Books, 1993.

O'Neill, Eugene (introduction by Christine Dymkowski). *Long Day's Journey Into Night*. London: Nick Hern Books, 2000.

O'Neill, Eugene. *A Moon for the Misbegotten*. London: Butler and Tanner Ltd, 1953.

Points, Jeremy. *Studying American Beauty*. Leighton Buzzard: Auteur, 2009.

Proulx, E. Annie. *The Shipping News*. London: Fourth Estate, 1993.

Rabe, David. *Hurlyburly*. New York: Grove Press Inc, 1985.

Rigby, Christopher. *Book of Lists: Over 500 Lists of Facts, Stats and Trivia*. Essex: Miles Kelly Publishing, 2005.

Ryan Hyde, Catherine. *Pay It Forward*. New York: Simon & Schuster, 1999.

Shaffer, Anthony. *Sleuth*. London: Marion Boyars, 1988.

Schiller, Friedrich (translated and introduced by F. J. Lamport). *The Robbers & Wallenstein*. Harmondsworth: Penguin, 1979.

Simon, Neil. *The Gingerbread Lady*. New York: Samuel French Inc, 1971.

Simon, Neil. *The Odd Couple*. New York: Samuel French Inc, 1966.

Simon, Neil. *Lost in Yonkers*. New York: Plume, 1993.

Thomson, David. *The New Biographical Dictionary of Film (Fourth Edition)*. London: Little Brown, 2003.

Tichler, Rosemarie, and Kaplan, Barrie Jay. *Actors At Work*. New York: Faber and Faber Limited, 2007.

Ulmer, James. *James Ulmer's Hollywood Hot List*. New York: St. Martin's Griffin, 2000.

# Filmography

*Albino Alligator* (1997), directed by Kevin Spacey, written by Christian Forte.

*American Beauty* (1999), directed by Sam Mendes, written by Alan Ball.

*The Apartment* (1960), directed by Billy Wilder, written by Billy Wilder and I.A.L. Diamond.

*Austin Powers in Goldmember* (2002), directed by Jay Roach, written by Mike Myers & Michael McCullers.

*Beyond the Sea* (2004), directed by Kevin Spacey, written by Kevin Spacey and Lewis Colick.

*The Big Kahuna* (2000), directed by John Swanbeck, written by Roger Rueff (based on his play *Hospitality Suite*).

*A Bug's Life* (1998), directed by John Lasseter and Andrew Stanton, story by John Lasseter and Andrew Stanton and Joe Ranft, screenplay by Andrew Stanton and Donald McEnery & Bob Shaw.

*Consenting Adults* (1992), directed by Alan J. Pakula, written by Matthew Chapman.

*Crime Story* (1987), episode "The Senator, the Movie Star, and the Mob," directed by John Nicolella, story by Peter Lance and Mark Rosner & Michael Mann, teleplay by Peter Lance.

*Dad* (1989), written and directed by Gary David Goldberg (based on the novel by William Wharton).

*Darrow* (1991), directed by John David Coles, story by William Schmidt, teleplay by William Schmidt and Stephen Stept.

*Edison* (2005), written and directed by David J. Burke.

*Fred Claus* (2007), directed by David Dobkin, story by Jessie Nelson and Dan Fogelman, screenplay by Dan Fogelman.

*Glengarry Glen Ross* (1992), directed by James Foley, written by David Mamet (based on his play).

*Heartburn* (1986), directed by Mike Nichols, written by Nora Ephron (based on her novel).

*Henry & June* (1990), directed by Philip Kaufman, written by Philip Kaufman & Rose Kaufman (based on the diaries of Anaïs Nin).

*Hurlyburly* (1998), directed by Anthony Drazan, written by David Rabe (based on his play).

*Iron Will* (1994), directed by Charles Haid, written by John Michael Hayes and Djordje Milicevic and Jeff Arch.

*K-Pax* (2001), directed by Ian Softley, written by Charles Leavitt (based on the novel by Gene Brewer).

*L.A. Confidential* (1997), directed by Curtis Hanson, written by Brian Helgeland & Curtis Hanson (based on the novel by James Ellroy).

*L.A. Confidential* (2003), pilot episode, directed by Eric Laneuville, written by Walon Green.

*The Life of David Gale* (2003), directed by Alan Parker, written by Charles Randolph.

*Long Day's Journey Into Night* (1987), directed by Jonathan Miller, written by Eugene O'Neill.

*Midnight in the Garden of Good and Evil* (1997), directed by Clint Eastwood, written by John Lee Hancock (based on the book by John Berendt).

*The Murder of Mary Phagan* (1988), directed by Billy Hale, story by Larry McMurtry, teleplay by Jeffrey Lane & George Stevens Jr.

*The Negotiator* (1998), directed by F. Gary Gray, written by James DeMonaco & Kevin Fox.

*Ordinary Decent Criminal* (2000), directed by Thaddeus O'Sullivan, written by Gerard Stembridge.

*Outbreak* (1995), directed by Wolfgang Petersen, written by Laurence Dworet & Robert Roy Pool.

*Pay It Forward* (2000), directed by Mimi Leder, written by Leslie Dixon (based on the novel by Catherine Ryan Hyde).

*Recount* (2008), directed by Jay Roach, written by Danny Strong.

*The Ref* (1994), directed by Ted Demme, story by Marie Weiss, screenplay by Richard LaGravenese and Marie Weiss.

*Rocket Gibraltar* (1988), directed by Daniel Petrie, written by Amos Poe.

*See No Evil, Hear No Evil* (1989), directed by Arthur Hillier, story by Earl Barret & Arne Sultan & Marvin Worth, screenplay by Earl Barret & Arne Sultan and Eliot Wald & Andrew Kurtzman and Gene Wilder.

*Se7en* (1995), directed by David Fincher, written by Andrew Kevin Walker.

*The Shipping News* (2001), directed by Lasse Hallström, written by Robert Nelson Jacobs (based on the novel by E. Annie Proulx).

*Superman Returns* (2006), directed by Bryan Singer, story by Bryan Singer & Michael Dougherty & Dan Harris, screenplay by Michael Dougherty & Dan Harris.

*Swimming With Sharks* (1994), written and directed by George Huang.

*Telstar* (2009), directed by Nick Moran, written by James Hicks and Nick Moran (inspired by the book *The Legendary Joe Meek* by John Repsch).

*A Time To Kill* (1996), directed by Joel Schumacher, written by Akiva Goldsman (based on the novel by John Grisham).

*21* (2008), directed by Robert Luketic, written by Peter Steinfeld and Allan Loeb (based on the book *Bringing Down The House* by Ben Mezrich).

*The United States of Leland* (2003), written and directed by Matthew Ryan Hoge.

*The Usual Suspects* (1995), directed by Bryan Singer, written by Christopher McQuarrie.

*Wiseguy* (1988), episodes "Fascination for the Flame" (directed by William A. Fraker, written by Stephen J. Cannell), "Smokey Mountain Requiem" (directed by Neill Fearnley, story by David J. Burke & Hans Tobeason, teleplay by David J. Burke), "Player to be Named Now" (directed by Ron Rapiel, written by Stephen Kronish), "Merchant of Death" (directed by William A. Fraker, written by Carol Mendelsohn), "Not for Nothing" (directed by Bill Corcoran, written by David J. Burke & Don Kurt), "The Squeeze" (directed by Bill Corcoran, written by Gina Wendkos), "Blood Dance" (directed by Kim Manners, written by Eric Blakeney).

*Working Girl* (1988), directed by Mike Nichols, written by Kevin Wade.

# Endnotes

1   Green, Jonathon. *Cassell's Dictionary of Slang*, p.1115.

2   Shaffer, Anthony. *Sleuth*, p.76.

3   Quoted in Fleming, Michael. February 2003. "The thinking person's sex symbol," *Movieline*.

4   As posted by Spacey, Kevin, on Twitter (www.twitter.com/kevinspacey), 29 October 2017.

5   Quoted in Allan, Vicky. 17 February 2002. "Unusual suspect," *Scotland on Sunday*.

6   Quoted in Bracchi, Paul. 20 April 2004. "Why is Spacey so secretive?" *The Daily Mail*.

7   A Google search conducted in July 2009 brought up 223 websites where Kevin's "real" name is given as "Kevin Matthew Fowler." See also Ulmer, James. *James Ulmer's Hollywood Hot List*, p.38; Rigby, Christopher. *Book of Lists*, p.229, and the venerable *Time Almanac*, p.70. Early in his career, the name "Spacey" was also incorrectly described as being Kevin's patchwork homage to actor Spencer Tracy.

8   Geoff's Social Security records show an even greater range of monikers: "Sep 1942: Name listed as THOMAS CORDEN LONGSHORE; Oct 1954: Name listed as THOMAS CORDEN FOWLER; Apr 1955: Name listed as BRECK FOWLER; Feb 1961: Name listed as THOMAS GEOFFREY FOWLER; 13 Jan 1993: Name listed as THOMAS G FOWLER."

9   Quoted in unknown. 3 September 1997. "'Confidential' commentary," *Spliced*.

10  Thomson, David. *The New Biographical Dictionary of Film*, p.826.

11  Quoted in Gumbel, Andrew. 5 October 2002. "Kevin Spacey: An enigma, even as he steps on to the political stage," *The Independent*.

12  This is how Spacey was once described by an *Entertainment Weekly* critic (Nashawaty, Chris. 7 August 1998. "Kevin Spacey and Samuel L. Jackson: the 25 Greatest Actors Of The '90s," *Entertainment Weekly*, issue 444). The allusion is to Dutch graphic artist M.C. Escher (1898-1972), best known for his visually paradoxical lithographs such as *Ascending and Descending* (1960) and *Waterfall* (1961). On detailed viewing, they prove to be geometrically impossible.

13 See, for example, Rafferty, Terrence. October 2000. "Kevin Spacey Needs A Hug," *GQ*; Frostrup, Mariella. 2 March 2003. "Anybody worth their salt feels like a fake most of the time," *The Observer*; Smith, David. 25 April 2004. "Spacey: face in the crowd," *The Observer*. Frostrup is particularly perceptive: "He's often quoted as saying that when he discovered acting, he finally learnt how to be himself. I suspect the reverse is true, that in acting he found a way of never having to be himself."

14 Christopher, James. 1 April 2002. "Ground control to major star," *The Times*.

15 Quoted in Junod, Tom. October 1997. "Kevin Spacey Has a Secret," *Esquire Magazine*.

16 See "John Graham Spacey" entry on the Internet Movie Database, www.imdb. com. The IMDB describes John Graham (born Henry John Spacey) as Kevin's "great-great-uncle," however this relationship is not supported by genealogical records and may be yet another example of Spacey misinformation–Randy recalls his mother (who was herself given to romancing the family background) mentioning the connection several years ago. "Officially" born on 8th August 1897, some sources give John Graham's date of birth as 8th August 1895: like many actors, he appears to have shaved a couple of years off his age on reaching Hollywood.

17 Bayard Cecil Fowler married Louella Officer in September 1927: they were together until his death in 1966, though Thomas Corden Geoffrey is his only known offspring. One of Bayard Cecil's British ancestors, Robert Hovenden (1495-1558), was also an ancestor of the author of this book, making Kevin Spacey and myself fourteenth cousins once removed.

18 Unknown. 2 March 1930. "Fowler-Longshore Wedding Saturday," *Casper Star Tribune*.

19 See Welch, Mike. Fall/Winter 2001/02. "Hide and Seek with Kevin Spacey," *Maxim*.

20 See Spacey, Kevin. September 2004. "Center Stage," *Condé Nast Traveller*.

21 Quoted in Ewing, Jack. *Spacey's Brother*, p.92.

22 Quoted in Ewing, Jack. *Spacey's Brother*, p.35.

23 Fowler, Kathleen. 24 April 1984. Letter to her "Dearest Children," courtesy Randy Fowler.

24 Fowler, Kathleen. 24 April 1984. Letter to her "Dearest Children," courtesy Randy Fowler.

25 Quoted in Leith, William. 16 February 2002. "Look, Dad, top of the world," *The Guardian*.

26 See Churcher, Sharon. 25 April 2004. "Kevin Spacey's father was a sexual monster," *The Mail on Sunday*. For additional biographical information on Geoff and Kathleen's early lives, see Ewing, Jack. *Spacey's Brother*, pp.21-44.

27 Quoted in Frostrup, Mariella. 2 March 2003. "Anybody worth their salt feels like a fake most of the time," *The Observer*.

28 Quoted in Raphael, Amy. March 2002. "Kevin Spacey, Comic Genius," *Esquire UK*.

29 Quoted in Frostrup, Mariella. 2 March 2003. "Anybody worth their salt feels like a fake most of the time," *The Observer*.

30 Quoted in Harper, Kenn. *Give Me My Father's Body*, p.xiii.

31 Quoted in Allan, Vicky. 17 February 2002. "Unusual suspect," *Scotland on Sunday*.

32 Fowler, Kathleen. 24 April 1984. Letter to her "Dearest Children," courtesy Randy Fowler.

33 Quoted in Frostrup, Mariella. 2 March 2003. "Anybody worth their salt feels like a fake most of the time," *The Observer*.

34 See Churcher, Sharon. 25 April 2004. "Kevin Spacey's father was a sexual monster," *The Mail on Sunday*.

35 Quoted in Ewing, Jack. *Spacey's Brother*, p.233.

36 Quoted in Fleming, Michael. October 1999. "Playboy Interview: Kevin Spacey," *Playboy Magazine*.

37 Fowler, Kathleen. 24 April 1984. Letter to her "Dearest Children," courtesy Randy Fowler. In April 1984, Randy called his father in an attempt to discuss the impact of the abuse he had suffered as a child on his adult relationships. Geoff cruelly told his son that the past "had nothing to do with the present" and that Randy couldn't hold him responsible for his current difficulties. Geoff subsequently informed Kathleen of the conversation, which prompted her to send a ten-page letter justifying the Fowlers' lifestyle and parenting techniques to each of their three "Dearest Children." See Ewing, Jack. *Spacey's Brother*, pp.209-212.

38 Quoted in Churcher, Sharon. 25 April 2004. "Kevin Spacey's father was a sexual monster," *The Mail on Sunday*.

39 Quoted in Ewing, Jack. *Spacey's Brother*, p.349.

40 See Ewing, Jack. *Spacey's Brother*, pp.103-104.

41 Quoted in Welch, Mike. Fall/Winter 2001/02. "Hide and Seek with Kevin Spacey," *Maxim*.

42 Quoted in Ewing, Jack. *Spacey's Brother*, pp.57-58.

43 Quoted in Ewing, Jack. *Spacey's Brother*, p.66.

44 Quoted in Churcher, Sharon. 25 April 2004. "Kevin Spacey's father was a sexual monster," *The Mail on Sunday*.

45 Quoted in Fischer, Paul. 20 October 2001. "The Alien World of Kevin Spacey," *Film Monthly*.

46 Quoted in Winningham, Mare. February 1997. "Driving Mr. Spacey," *Interview Magazine*.

47 The following account (from a 2001 interview with Spacey) is fairly representative: "When I was about nine or 10 I went through a time of real rebellion within my family. I was mad, had no focus and was interested in nothing at all. I started to play with matches, caused trouble and did stupid things that kids should not do. As a result, my parents decided to send me to military school. I stayed there for a year or so and then got thrown out because I got into a fight. It was not a fair fight and I did what was right, but they had rules that if you were involved in trouble of any kind you had to go. It was fortuitous. I went back to public [state] school and some teachers turned me on to theatre and acting. That was the key moment in my life." Quoted in Pearce, Garth. 14 January 2001. "American Everyman," *Scotland on Sunday*. Spacey also claims to have won a leadership medal shortly before his "expulsion," "the first award" he ever received. See Winningham, Mare. February 1997. "Driving Mr. Spacey," *Interview Magazine*.

48 See Ewing, Jack. *Spacey's Brother*, p.55.

49 See Ewing, Jack. *Spacey's Brother*, pp.93-94.

50 Quoted in Ewing, Jack. *Spacey's Brother*, p.103.

51 Fowler, Kathleen. 24 April 1984. Letter to her "Dearest Children," courtesy Randy Fowler.

52 See Ewing, Jack. *Spacey's Brother*, p.104. The Academy later re-opened and continued to admit students for a number of years, but is now defunct.

53 Quoted in Ewing, Jack. *Spacey's Brother*, p.417.

54 Spacey, Kevin. September 2004. "Center Stage," *Condé Nast Traveller*.

55 See Ewing, Jack. *Spacey's Brother*, p.55.

56 See Ewing, Jack. *Spacey's Brother*, pp.106-107. Julie and Ian–who have two adult children, Ingrid (born 1975) and Colin (born 1981)–moved back to the U.S. in 1974 and now reside in California.

57 Ewing, Jack. *Spacey's Brother*, p.107.

58 Quoted in Martin, Tricia. 21 April 2001. "A law unto himself–Drama," *The Sun*.

59 Nor was the Old Vic the only theatre that Spacey contributed monies to. In May 2000, he put up enough capital to allow the off-Broadway revival of Lee Blessing's 1989 play *Cobb* (about the baseball player Ty Cobb) to continue running for another two weeks when it was on the verge of closing, and later helped finance a commercial production at the Lucille Lortel Theater in Greenwich Village. Larry Hirschhorn, artistic director of the company that staged the off-Broadway show, related how he received a call from Spacey after the actor attended a performance. "He said: 'You can't close it, it's too good. How much would it cost to keep open?' I told him, and I got a check the next day. I don't even know the guy..." Quoted in Pogrebin, Robin. 28 November 2000. "Spacey Putting His Money Where His Heart Has Been," *The New York Times*. Kevin is also a prominent supporter of the Screen Actors' Guild,

donating several hundred thousand dollars to the relief fund during a period of pay strikes in 2000 and 2001.

60 Quoted in Labi, Aisha. 9 February 2003. "Help Us Fix The Roof," *Time Magazine.*

61 Quoted in Grant, Steve. 6 August 2000. "The Lambeth talk: Theatre," *The Sunday Times.*

62 Or as Spacey-as-Spacey (when defending his friend, lawyer and then-Prime Minister's wife Cherie Blair, over allegations that she had not been "entirely honest" over her business dealings with convicted conman Peter Foster) said: "So she lied? We all lie. We all lie all the time. Big deal!" Quoted in Walker, Tim. 15 December 2002. "Cherie's defender," *The Sunday Telegraph.*

63 Quoted in Allan, Vicky. 17 February 2002. "Unusual suspect," *Scotland on Sunday.* Spacey's apparent shyness–which led one group of childhood acquaintances to nickname him "Moody" (see Raphael, Amy. March 2002. "Kevin Spacey, Comic Genius," *Esquire UK),* accompanied by an ability to blend into the background, may well have been a safeguard against his father. As Jessica Berens noted in a 2004 profile of the actor that cited Randy's *Mail on Sunday* interview, "invisibility is useful in scenarios where protection is of paramount importance." Berens, Jessica. 11 November 2004. "Lost in Spacey," *The Telegraph.*

64 See Ewing, Jack. *Spacey's Brother,* p.101.

65 Quoted in Passero, Kathy. February 2003. "Kevin Spacey: a Candid Conversation," *Biography.*

66 Quoted in Tichler, Rosemarie, and Kaplan, Barry Jay. *Actors at Work,* pp.308-309.

67 See Ewing, Jack. *Spacey's Brother,* p.117.

68 Quoted in Rader, Dotson. 24 October 1999. "A Glimpse of How Beautiful Life Can Be," *Parade.*

69 Quoted in Pearce, Garth. 14 January 2001. "American Everyman," *Scotland on Sunday.*

70 Quoted in Leith, William. 16 February 2002. "Look, Dad, top of the world," *The Guardian.*

71 Fowler, Kathleen. 24 April 1984. Letter to her "Dearest Children," courtesy Randy Fowler.

72 Quoted in Mills, Nancy. 18 December 2001. "Heavy Spacey," *The New York Daily News.*

73 Quoted in Mutti-Mewse, Austin. Fall 2003. "Inner Spacey," *Privatair Magazine,* issue 10.

74 Quoted in Rader, Dotson. 24 October 1999. "A Glimpse of How Beautiful Life Can Be," *Parade.*

75  Quoted in Tayman, John. 10 June 1991. "Man on the Edge," *People Magazine*, volume 35, no.22.

76  Winningham received an Oscar nomination (though not a win) for her role in the film *Georgia* in 1996, the same year as Spacey got his first nod for *The Usual Suspects*. The actress promptly phoned Kevin and said: "This is Maria. Is this Captain Von Trapp? Congratulations!" Quoted in Weinraub, Bernard. 14 February 1996. "Oscar Nominations Are Just One Surprise After Another," *The New York Times*.

77  Quoted in Ewing, Jack. *Spacey's Brother*, p.128.

78  Quoted by Spacey, Kevin, during an appearance on "Enough Rope with Andrew Denton," ABC Australia, 10 July 2006.

79  Quoted in Leith, William. 16 February 2002. "Look, Dad, top of the world," *The Guardian*.

80  Quoted in Fleming, Michael. October 1999. "Playboy Interview: Kevin Spacey," *Playboy Magazine*.

81  Kevin has also done his "funny voices" on everything from *Wiseguy* to *Beyond the Sea*, as well as several chat shows and even a political conference. He is himself now a favourite target of impressionists, notably Scouse comedian Peter Serafinowicz, whose sinister "Acting Masterclass" take-off of Spacey auditioning a group of terrified students—"don't take it personal, I just hate women"—is pure cold perfection.

82  See Ewing, Jack. *Spacey's Brother*, pp.129-130.

83  Quoted in Gray, Marianne. December 1998. "If The Negotiator is anything to go by, you don't want to get on the wrong side of stars Kevin Spacey or Samuel L. Jackson," *Film Review*.

84  Quoted in Dietch Rohrer, Trish. May 1999. "Unusual Suspect," *Elle*.

85  Quoted in Fleming, Michael. October 1999. "Playboy Interview: Kevin Spacey," *Playboy Magazine*.

86  Kevin has, however, explicitly referred to "Spacey" as being "my mother's maiden name" in at least one interview: see Mutti-Mewse, Austin. Fall 2003. "Inner Spacey," *Privatair Magazine*, issue 10.

87  See Ewing, Jack. *Spacey's Brother*, p.40.

88  See Fowler, Kathleen. 24 April 1984. Letter to her "Dearest Children," courtesy Randy Fowler.

89  Unknown. 26 March 1966. "Bayard Fowler obituary," *Times Advocate*.

90  Quoted in Leith, William. 16 February 2002. "Look, Dad, top of the world," *The Guardian*. Allen Knutson died in 1970, outliving his former wife Harriet by five years.

91  Quoted in White, Lesley. 19 December 1999. "Spacey's Odyssey," *The Sunday Times Magazine*.

92  Quoted in Ramos, Steve. 16 March 2000. "City Beat's Oscar Pick: Best Actor Nominee: Kevin Spacey," *City Beat.*

93  See Ewing, Jack. *Spacey's Brother*, pp.131-132.

94  Quoted in Dietch Rohrer, Trish. May 1999. "Unusual Suspect," *Elle.*

95  Quoted in Passero, Kathy. February 2003. "Kevin Spacey: a Candid Conversation," *Biography.* Spacey also employed artifice to sneak into less glamorous places. "I used to borrow a tuxedo from the costume department at [Juilliard], telling them I needed it for a Noel Coward scene in class," he informed a group of graduates from the American Academy of Dramatic Arts in 1999. "Then I would go to whatever convention they were having at the Sheraton Hotel–Dentists of the Midwest, Industrial Lubricants Spring Gala–because they always had a free buffet. So I would be stuffing my pockets with bread, saying, 'Yeah, that new molar bit is really good!'" Quoted in Rush, George, and Molloy, Joanna. 29 April 1999. "Who are those masked men? The Jacksons," *The New York Daily News.*

96  Quoted in Griffin, Nancy. October 1999. "No more Mr. Bad Guy," *Los Angeles Magazine.*

97  Quoted in O'Donoghue, Anna. September 2007. "Kevin Spacey Urges Students To Act From the Heart," *The Juilliard Journal.*

98  Quoted in Hamilton, William. *Blessed*, pp.18-19.

99  The amount of money Spacey borrowed from Kilmer Sr. is also a matter of dispute. Val insists the sum was "like $18,000" of which only $1000 was ever returned, while Spacey claims it was $800 and has been repaid in full. See unknown. 5 October 2002. "Saturday Profile," *The Scotsman.*

100  Quoted in Hadleigh, Boze. *Celebrity Diss & Tell*, p.241.

101  Quoted in Spencer, Kathryn, Carpenter, Julie and Bohdanowicz, Kate. 13 May 2005. "Day and Night," *The Express.*

102  Quoted in Model, Betsy. January/February 2002. "American Paradox," *Cigar Aficionado.* Eventually, after winning his second Oscar, Spacey was awarded an honorary degree from the school.

103  Quoted in Tichler, Rosemarie, and Kaplan, Barry Jay. *Actors at Work*, p.312.

104  Quoted in Kennedy, Dana. 12 November 1992. "Spacey's Acting Roles Are No Joke To Him," *The Kokomo Tribune.*

105  Quoted in Fleming, Michael. October 1999. "Playboy Interview: Kevin Spacey," *Playboy Magazine.*

106  Quoted in Thorncroft, Antony. 2 September 2000. "'Theatre's more important to me than acting': Lunch with the FT," *The Financial Times.*

107  Quoted in Rader, Dotson. 24 October 1999. "A Glimpse of How Beautiful Life Can Be," *Parade.*

108  See Ewing, Jack. *Spacey's Brother*, p.183.

109  Quoted in Haun, Harry. April 1999. "A Pipe Dream Realized," *Playbill.*

110 Quoted in Fleming, Michael. October 1999. "Playboy Interview: Kevin Spacey," *Playboy Magazine*.

111 Spacey has related this story to at least two publications: see Stahl, Jerry. October 1996. "Hollywood's King of Cool," *Buzz Magazine*, and White, Lesley. 19 December 1999. "Spacey's Odyssey," *The Sunday Times Magazine*.

112 Fowler, Kathleen. 24 April 1984. Letter to her "Dearest Children," courtesy Randy Fowler.

113 Quoted in Ewing, Jack. *Spacey's Brother*, p.344. Spacey's straitened circumstances do appear to be supported by other sources, however. A 2004 *Observer* article referred to an (unnamed) friend of Kevin "remembering seeing Spacey on the streets of New York with his dog, unable to buy the dog a hamburger because 'he didn't have two cents to rub together'" (Smith, David. 25 April 2004. "Spacey: face in the crowd," *The Observer*); perhaps Kevin concealed his lack of other funds from his mother?

114 Unknown. 29 July 1981. "Norma Louise Longshore obituary," *The Calgary Herald*.

115 See Ewing, Jack. *Spacey's Brother*, p.187. Kathleen's 1984 letter listed several possible reasons for Norma's decision to exclude her eldest son from her will, including the confrontation over Geoff's missing Army payments and the fact that the Fowlers had never been able to visit the Longshores in Canada as they could not afford to fund the trip, though–perhaps significantly–she did not mention Norma's disapproval of Geoff's political allegiances. See Fowler, Kathleen. 24 April 1984. Letter to her "Dearest Children," courtesy Randy Fowler.

116 Beaufort, John. 26 September 1982. "Ibsen on Broadway," *The Sunday Intelligencer*.

117 Gussow, Mel. 31 August 1982. "Theater: Liv Ullmann is the star of 'Ghosts'," *The New York Times*.

118 Sharbutt, Jay. 1 September 1982. "A tragic 'Ghosts', *The Capital*.

119 Quoted in Rafferty, Terrence. October 2000. "Kevin Spacey Needs A Hug," *GQ*.

120 Quoted in Fleming, Michael. October 1999. "Playboy Interview: Kevin Spacey," *Playboy Magazine*.

121 Quoted in Stahl, Jerry. October 1996. "Hollywood's King of Cool," *Buzz Magazine*.

122 Quoted in Smith, David. 25 April 2004. "Spacey: face in the crowd," *The Observer*.

123 Palmer, Paul. 22 April 2004. "Kevin's London beauties," *The Evening Standard*.

124 Smith, David. 25 April 2004. "Spacey: face in the crowd," *The Observer*.

125 Quoted in Kennedy, Dana. 12 November 1992. "Spacey's Acting Roles Are No Joke To Him," *The Kokomo Tribune*.

126 See Ewing, Jack. *Spacey's Brother*, p.208.

127 See Ewing, Jack. *Spacey's Brother*, p.221.

128 See Ewing, Jack. *Spacey's Brother*, p.227.

129 Quoted in unknown. 12 March 2000. "Spacey and Lemmon: A Couple of Winners Talk Awards and Acting," *The Sunday New York Times*.

130 Quoted in Ginsberg, Merle. November 2001. "Inner Spacey," *W Magazine*.

131 Miller gave lectures on two consecutive nights. Spacey, who had read in *The Village Voice* that the director was coming to New York, realised he must be casting for *Journey* and bought tickets for both events in the hope of meeting him.

132 Quoted in Ginsberg, Merle. July 1998. "Exploring Spacey," *W Magazine*.

133 Quoted in an audio interview included on the DVD release of *Long Day's Journey Into Night*, 2005.

134 Spacey, Kevin. September & October 2004. "One Life to Give," *AARP Magazine*.

135 See Dietch Rohrer, Trish. May 1999. "Unusual Suspect," *Elle*.

136 Quoted in Celeste, Eric. 15 March 2008. "The Unusual Suspect," *American Way Magazine*. When discussing this encounter with Lemmon during a 2000 interview, Spacey did not mention the older actor's supposed words of praise.

137 See Lemmon, Chris. *A Twist of Lemmon*, p.x.

138 Spacey, Kevin. September & October 2004. "One Life to Give," *AARP Magazine*. Spacey had previously named the exact date of the trip as "December 12, 1974," meaning that he would actually have been fifteen-and-a-half at the time. See unknown. 12 March 2000. "Spacey and Lemmon: A Couple of Winners Talk Awards and Acting," *The Sunday New York Times*.

139 Quoted in Smith, David. 25 April 2004. "Spacey: face in the crowd," *The Observer*.

140 Quoted in Fleming, Michael. October 1999. "Playboy Interview: Kevin Spacey," *Playboy Magazine*.

141 Quoted in Warren, Jane. 18 August 2009. "Hotel for dogs," *The Express*.

142 Quoted in unknown. 12 March 2000. "Spacey and Lemmon: A Couple of Winners Talk Awards and Acting," *The Sunday New York Times*.

143 Bloom, Steven F. Summer-Fall 1986. "Review of O'Neill plays in performance: Long Day's Journey Into Night," *The Eugene O'Neill Newsletter*, vol. X, No. 2.

144 O'Neill, Eugene. *Long Day's Journey Into Night*, p.6.

145 Peter, John. 10 August 1986. "Price of playing to the gallery," *The Sunday Times*.

146 Quoted in Poe, Amos. Fall 1989. "Kevin Spacey," *Bomb Magazine*, issue 29. Despite the indifferent reaction to the play from American critics, Miller, Lemmon, Gallagher and Bethel Leslie (as mother Mary) all received Tony nominations.

147  Quoted in Wolf, Matt. 5 September 2004. "He has left Hollywood behind to try to stage a revival of the Old Vic's fortunes–Kevin Spacey," *The Sunday Times*.

148  *Mary Phagan*, which was based on a true story, is set in Atlanta in 1913 and concerns a Jewish factory owner, Leo Frank (played by *Journey's* Peter Gallagher) who is wrongly accused of the murder of one of his young employees by a group of anti-Semitic officials headed by solicitor general Hugh Dorsey (Richard Jordan). As Wes Brent, an ambitious young reporter, Spacey initially supports Dorsey in generating a media sensation around the trial, but belatedly develops a conscience after being befriended by charismatic private eye William Burns (Paul Dooley)–"If you're as smart–or as sad–as I think you are, and I don't care which, well, I thought you might need [a friend] too," Burns cautions. Governor John Slaton (Lemmon) commutes Frank's execution to a life sentence, which leads to several revenge attacks on Jewish businesses in the state. Frank is subsequently kidnapped from prison and lynched by a misguided mob calling themselves "The Knights of Mary Phagan," while the true perpetrator (the factory's alcoholic janitor, who is black) escapes with a lesser charge of assisting Frank in concealing Mary's body.

149  Spacey, Kevin. September & October 2004. "One Life to Give," *AARP Magazine*.

150  Quoted in Armstrong, Stephen. 30 March 2008. "Why Kevin Spacey has never been happier," *The Sunday Times*.

151  Quoted in Fuller, Nick. *Call Me Bud*, p.102.

152  Quoted by Spacey, Kevin, in an audio interview included on the DVD release of *Long Day's Journey Into Night*, 2005.

153  Quoted in Fuller, Nick. *Call Me Bud*, p.127.

154  Quoted in Stahl, Jerry. October 1996. "Hollywood's King of Cool," *Buzz Magazine*.

155  Quoted by Spacey, Kevin, during an appearance on "Connie Chung Tonight," CNN, 30 December 2002.

156  As posted in answer to the question "What is the purpose of TriggerStreet.com?" on the official website, www.triggerstreet.com.

157  Quoted in Tayman, John. 10 June 1991. "Man on the Edge," *People Magazine*, volume 35, no.22.

158  Quoted in Harris, Mark. 7 June 1991. "Kevin Spacey Holds Court," *Entertainment Weekly*, issue 69.

159  Quoted in Fleming, Michael. October 1999. "Playboy Interview: Kevin Spacey," *Playboy Magazine*.

160  Quoted in White, Lesley. 19 December 1999. "Spacey's Odyssey," *The Sunday Times Magazine*.

161 Quoted in O'Haire, Patricia. 8 January 1996. "A film bad guy's arresting roles: critics love his creeps, but Kevin Spacey's acting on a new plan," *The New York Daily News*.

162 Quoted in Poe, Amos. Fall 1989. "Kevin Spacey," *Bomb Magazine*, issue 29.

163 Quoted in Weinstock, Jeff. Summer 1998. "The spin on Kevin Spacey," *Smoke*.

164 Quoted in Tichler, Rosemarie, and Kaplan, Barry Jay. *Actors at Work*, p.320.

165 See Rayner, Richard. 1 October 1999. "The Spaceman Cometh," *Harper's Bazaar*.

166 Davies, Howard, quoted in Benedict, David. 25 April 2004. "Kevin confidential," *The Independent on Sunday*.

167 Quoted in White, Lesley. 19 December 1999. "Spacey's Odyssey," *The Sunday Times Magazine*.

168 Quoted in Fleming, Michael. October 1999. "Playboy Interview: Kevin Spacey," *Playboy Magazine*.

169 Quoted in Welch, Mike. Fall/Winter 2001/02. "Hide and Seek with Kevin Spacey," *Maxim*.

170 Quoted in Poe, Amos. Fall 1989. "Kevin Spacey," *Bomb Magazine*, issue 29.

171 Quoted in Fleming, Michael. October 1999. "Playboy Interview: Kevin Spacey," *Playboy Magazine*.

172 Quoted in Poe, Amos. Fall 1989. "Kevin Spacey," *Bomb Magazine*, issue 29.

173 Mel's demise could perhaps be compared to Oswald's in *Ghosts*. Fearing the mental collapse his inherited syphilis will inevitably lead to, Oswald asks his mother to lend him "a helping hand" to take an overdose of morphine before his next blackout: "Mother, give me the sun…" he pleads as madness descends. Ibsen, Henrik. *Four Major Plays*, pp.162 & 163.

174 Quoted in Werts, Diane. 31 December 2004. "DVDs Show How Crime Did Pay For Future Stars," *Newsday*.

175 Quoted in Werts, Diane. 31 December 2004. "DVDs Show How Crime Did Pay For Future Stars," *Newsday*. Jim Profit (played by Adrian Pasdar), the psychotic, amoral anti-hero of the short-lived 1996 drama series *Profit*, on which Cannell served as executive producer, was reputedly "inspired" by Mel.

176 Quoted in Poe, Amos. Fall 1989. "Kevin Spacey," *Bomb Magazine*, issue 29.

177 Quoted in Poe, Amos. Fall 1989. "Kevin Spacey," *Bomb Magazine*, issue 29.

178 See Vawter, Ron, quoted in Hadleigh, Boze. *Celebrity Diss & Tell*, p.189.

179 Quoted in Leyva, Ric. 24 July 1996. "Star Watch: Kevin Spacey Won't Let Success Spoil the Fun," *The Standard Times*.

180 Grant, Richard E. *With Nails*, pp.74-75.

181 Grant, Richard E. *With Nails*, pp.85-86. After being offered a provisional role in his next movie by the director Robert Altman, Grant muses: "I feel poised to give this good news to Kevin, knowing that he will dispatch himself like an Exocet missile in Mr. Altman's direction within a sec" (p.96). Ironically

enough, Spacey's eventual Old Vic collaboration with Altman (who according to Spacey's acerbic Buddy Ackerman character "couldn't direct his way out of a paper bag") proved a disaster.

182 Spacey, Kevin. 26 June 2000. "Neil Simon at the Neil Simon The Playwright's The Thing II," *Playbill.*

183 Kevin himself left the show in early August 1991, to film his part in *Glengarry Glen Ross.*

184 Simon, Neil. *Lost in Yonkers*, p.57.

185 Simon, Neil. *Lost in Yonkers*, p.61.

186 Simon, Neil. *Lost in Yonkers*, p.87.

187 Simon, Neil. *Lost in Yonkers*, p.88.

188 Rich, Frank. 22 February 1991. "Review/Theater; Simon on Love Denied," *The New York Times.*

189 Quoted in Tayman, John. 10 June 1991. "Man on the Edge," *People Magazine*, volume 35, no.22. *The Odd Couple*, first performed in 1965, is a comic tale of two mismatched men–sloppy chauvinist Oscar and fastidious hypochondriac Felix–who are forced to share an apartment following their respective marital splits. After a successful Broadway run (the play was directed by *Hurlyburly*'s Mike Nichols), it was adapted for the screen in 1968, with Walter Matthau reprising his stage role, starring as Oscar alongside Spacey mentor Jack Lemmon as Felix: this version was helmed by *Lost in Yonkers*'s Gene Saks.

190 Spacey, Kevin. 26 June 2000. "Neil Simon at the Neil Simon The Playwright's The Thing II," *Playbill.*

191 Simon, Neil. *The Gingerbread Lady*, pp.16-17.

192 In an odd twist of fate, Dreyfuss (along with Kevin's former Juilliard classmate Elizabeth McGovern) would be directed by Spacey in the world premiere of Joe Sutton's *Complicit* at the Old Vic in early 2009. His participation in the play was subject to some controversy owing to his use of an earpiece on stage, allegedly because of his inability to learn his lines in time.

193 Quoted in Fleming, Michael. October 1999. "Playboy Interview: Kevin Spacey," *Playboy Magazine*. Seven years later Spacey appeared in–and co-produced–the similarly themed *The Big Kahuna*, another sharply scripted tale of seller intrigue. Set in the drab hospitality suite of a Kansas hotel, *Kahuna* was also based on a play–*Hospitality Suite* by Roger Rueff, a former chemical engineer whom Spacey had earlier helped secure an agent for. As cynical lubricant salesman Larry Mann, Kevin is in his element, his stage training clearly in evidence in both his effortless delivery of Larry's long, dry monologues–"Now it's the days of Larry and Phil–Phil and Larry–and Bob–three guys who are about to be royally fucked up the ass"–and his intense rage later in the film as he confronts the naïve Bob (Peter Facinelli) over his blindly-parroted religious faith. As one contemporary critic noted: "This is the Kevin Spacey we all love

to love: voluble, fast, funny, with a verbal dexterity miles beyond that of any other American actor. He doesn't read dialogue, he toys with it, diddles with it, makes it dance loops in his mouth, ultimately spits it out in lacy filigrees or bubbles with bubbles inside." Hunter, Stephen. 12 May 2000. "Big Kahuna: A Well-Oiled Act," *The Washington Post.*

194 Quoted in Fleming, Michael. November 2002. "The Most Daring Director in Hollywood," *Movieline.* Ironically, the actor eventually cast, Matt McCoy, was scarcely better known. Hanson finally secured Spacey's services five years later for *L.A. Confidential*, in which McCoy played a small supporting role.

195 Quoted in Bagley, Christopher. October 1992. "Cameos: actor Kevin Spacey," *Premiere.*

196 Spacey employed a similar strategy to effect Lester's physical transformation for *American Beauty*, installing a personal gym in a trailer near the film set.

197 Hinson, Hal. 16 October 1992. "Consenting Adults," *The Washington Post.*

198 Quoted in Armstrong, Stephen. 30 March 2008. "Why Kevin Spacey has never been happier," *The Sunday Times.*

199 Quoted in Fleming, Michael. October 1999. "Playboy Interview: Kevin Spacey," *Playboy Magazine.*

200 See Ewing, Jack. *Spacey's Brother*, pp.283-286.

201 Variety staff. Posted 6 January 1993. "Obituary: Thomas Geoffrey Fowler," *Variety.*

202 Unknown. 28 December 1992. "Thomas Geoffrey Fowler obituary," *The Atlanta Constitution.*

203 Quoted in Fleming, Michael. October 1999. "Playboy Interview: Kevin Spacey," *Playboy Magazine.*

204 Quoted in Brown, Mick. 9 August 1997. "Seriously Spacey," *The Telegraph.*

205 Quoted in White, Lesley. 19 December 1999. "Spacey's Odyssey," *The Sunday Times Magazine.*

206 Quoted in Leith, William. 16 February 2002. "Look, Dad, top of the world," *The Guardian.*

207 Spacey, Kevin. September & October 2004. "One Life to Give," *AARP Magazine.*

208 Quoted in Welch, Mike. Fall/Winter 2001/02. "Hide and Seek with Kevin Spacey," *Maxim.*

209 Quoted in Mills, Nancy. 18 December 2001. "Heavy Spacey," *The New York Daily News.*

210 Quoted in Frostrup, Mariella. 2 March 2003. "Anybody worth their salt feels like a fake most of the time," *The Observer.*

211 Quoted in Turner, Janice. August 2006. "And Now For The Bad Guy," *Elle.*

212 Quoted in de Rakoff, Sophie. March 1999. "The Nice Man Cometh," *Paper Magazine.*

213 Quoted in Frostrup, Mariella. 2 March 2003. "Anybody worth their salt feels like a fake most of the time," *The Observer*.

214 Quoted in Stahl, Jerry. October 1996. "Hollywood's King of Cool," *Buzz Magazine*.

215 Fowler, Kathleen. 24 April 1984. Letter to her "Dearest Children," courtesy Randy Fowler.

216 See Stahl, Jerry. October 1996. "Hollywood's King of Cool," *Buzz Magazine*.

217 Quoted in Ewing, Jack. *Spacey's Brother*, p.64.

218 Quoted in Leith, William.16 February 2002. "Look, Dad, top of the world," *The Guardian*. Spacey was equally unwilling to reveal any more details about the mysterious book five years later: "When [Geoff] passed, in going through his office I found out what he was doing because he never let any of us read it–he never thought it was good enough...He was writing a novel, the great novel. And it's 16 volumes, a monster. [What was it about?] That would be telling. But some day, who knows, maybe it will find a life." Quoted in Pryor, Cathy. 18 February 2007. "Watch this Spacey," *The Independent on Sunday*.

219 Quoted in Spector, Adam. 2 April 2004. "Adam's Rib: Thirty Minutes with Matthew Ryan Hoge," *The Washington DC Film Society Newsletter*.

220 Chekhov, Anton. *Four Plays*, p.56.

221 Quoted in unknown. February 2005. "Passion Players–*Premiere* Celebrates The Most Compelling Performances of 2004," *Premiere*.

222 Quoted in Bliss, Sara. May 2007. "The Drama King," *Gotham*.

223 Quoted in Raphael, Amy. March 2002. "Kevin Spacey, Comic Genius," *Esquire UK*.

224 Quoted in Churcher, Sharon. 25 April 2004. "Kevin Spacey's father was a sexual monster," The Mail on Sunday.

225 Fowler, Kathleen. 24 April 1984. Letter to her "Dearest Children," courtesy Randy Fowler.

226 Quoted in Baxter, Sarah. 6 October 2002. "Spacey invader–Focus," *The Sunday Times*.

227 Quoted in Baxter, Sarah. 6 October 2002. "Spacey invader–Focus," *The Sunday Times*.

228 Quoted in Palmer, Paul. 22 April 2004. "Kevin's London beauties," *The Evening Standard*.

229 Quoted in Palmer, Alun. 23 June 2009. "Part of me feels British now but the knife crime here is shocking," *The Daily Mirror*.

230 Spacey had been friendly with Blair and his wife Cherie for some years–he was one of the first celebrities invited to 10 Downing Street (Blair's political residence) after the latter's election in May 1997. When they appeared as fellow guests on Michael Parkinson's BBC chat show in March 2006, the two shared an easy chemistry–at one point a snickering Tony even patted Kevin's knee.

231 See Ewing, Jack. *Spacey's Brother*, p.57.

232 Spacey later played Henry Drummond, a character based on the elder Darrow, in Jerome Lawrence and Robert Edwin Lee's play *Inherit The Wind*, which opened at the Old Vic in September 2009. Ten years before, Jack Lemmon had won a Golden Globe for his portrayal of Drummond in a TV movie version of the play. Drummond has also been depicted on screen by Spacey favourites Spencer Tracy and Jason Robards.

233 In the original source novel, the teacher (here, a black man named Reuben St. Clair–the part was originally offered to Denzel Washington) received his wounds in Vietnam, and the change does not work in the story's favour. The parking lot scene in which Spacey recounts the story of his disfiguration to girlfriend Arlene (Helen Hunt) is so badly staged that it comes across as trite and over-the-top rather than poignant. A generally well-acted film, *Pay It Forward* is ruined by such poor set pieces. The ending, in which hundreds of candle-bearing followers of the "pay it [a good deed] forward" concept stage a vigil to Arlene's murdered son (Haley Joel Osment) outside her home as "Calling All Angels" plays into the closing credits, is even worse. As one contemporary reviewer noted: "There is either cynicism of a baroque order operating or a heavy-glucose earnestness close to idiocy. In a ghastly way it's mesmerising, like witnessing a mass suicide." Unknown. 25 January 2001. "Killed off by kindness: Pay It Forward," *The Scotsman*.

234 The source novel reveals that his initials are "R.G.," however it is not clear what "R.G." stands for and he is always referred to by his surname, perhaps to reinforce his drab personality.

235 Quoted in Leith, William. 16 February 2002. "Look, Dad, top of the world," *The Guardian*.

236 Quoted in Chetwynd, Josh. 27 August 2001. "Spacey savors 'Shipping News' role," *USA Today* online.

237 Quoted in Steinberg, Scott. January 2002. "Kevin Spacey–the king of cool?" *Insite Magazine*.

238 Quoted in Mutti-Mewse, Austin. Fall 2003. "Inner Spacey," *Privatair Magazine*, issue 10.

239 Quoted in Raphael, Amy. March 2002. "Kevin Spacey, Comic Genius," *Esquire UK*.

240 Quoted in Rayner, Richard. 1 October 1999. "The Spaceman Cometh," *Harper's Bazaar*. In his Academy Award acceptance speech for *Beauty*, Kevin thanked Lemmon for providing the inspiration for his performance and dedicated the Oscar to him.

241 Ball, Alan. *American Beauty*, pp.101-102.

242 Quoted in Chumo II, Peter N. January/February 2000. "American Beauty: An Interview with Alan Ball," *Creative Screenwriting Magazine*, no.29.

243 Quoted in Tayman, John. 10 June 1991. "Man on the Edge," *People Magazine*, volume 35, no.22.

244 *Exceptional Clearance*, the story of a vampiric serial killer on a revenge mission against New York City's police force, contains a minor character called "Andy Fowler"–one letter away from Kevin's brother's name.

245 The film was given the appalling title *Hostile Hostages* for its British cinema release, which probably contributed to its lukewarm reception at the box office.

246 Bernard, Jami. 9 March 1994. "The Ref: Review," *The New York Daily News*.

247 Gleiberman, Owen. 19 May 1995. "Swimming With the Sharks," *Entertainment Weekly*, issue 275.

248 Maslin, Janet. 21 April 1995. "Film Review: Getting Even in Hollywood Can Be Fun," *The New York Times*.

249 Raphael, Amy. March 2002. "Kevin Spacey, Comic Genius," *Esquire UK*.

250 McQuarrie, Christopher. *The Usual Suspects*, p.13.

251 Quoted in unknown. 8 September 1995. "Closing in on the leading 'suspect,'" *Entertainment Weekly*, issue 291.

252 Quoted in Winningham, Mare. February 1997. "Driving Mr. Spacey," *Interview Magazine*.

253 Larsen, Ernest. *BFI Modern Classics: The Usual Suspects*, p.54.

254 James, Caryn. 1 September 1995. "Critic's Choice/Film; Of Labyrinthine Plots, Flair and Slick Action," *The New York Times*.

255 Travers, Peter. 7 September 1995. "The Usual Suspects," *Rolling Stone*.

256 Quoted in Nashawaty, Chris. 7 August 1998. "Kevin Spacey and Samuel L. Jackson: the 25 Greatest Actors Of The '90s," *Entertainment Weekly*, issue 444.

257 Quoted in O'Haire, Patricia. 8 January 1996. "A film bad guy's arresting roles: critics love his creeps, but Kevin Spacey's acting on a new plan," *The New York Daily News*.

258 Quoted in Fleming, Michael. October 1999. "Playboy Interview: Kevin Spacey," *Playboy Magazine*.

259 See Ewing, Jack. *Spacey's Brother*, p.354.

260 Quoted in Grimes, William. 26 March 1996. "Gibson Best Director for 'Braveheart,' Best Film," *The New York Times*.

261 Quoted in Tayman, John. 10 June 1991. "Man on the Edge," *People Magazine*, volume 35, no.22.

262 Quoted in Fleming, Michael. October 1999. "Playboy Interview: Kevin Spacey," *Playboy Magazine*.

263 Tayman, John. 10 June 1991. "Man on the Edge," *People Magazine*, volume 35, no.22.

264 Junod, Tom. October 1997. "Kevin Spacey Has a Secret," *Esquire Magazine*.

265 Berendt, John. *Midnight in the Garden of Good and Evil*, p.3.

266 Quoted in Junod, Tom. October 1997. "Kevin Spacey Has a Secret," *Esquire Magazine.*

267 Junod, Tom. October 1997. "Kevin Spacey Has a Secret," *Esquire Magazine.*

268 Quoted in Fleming, Michael. October 1999. "Playboy Interview: Kevin Spacey," *Playboy Magazine.*

269 Quoted in Fleming, Michael. October 1999. "Playboy Interview: Kevin Spacey," *Playboy Magazine.*

270 Quoted in Pogrebin, Robin. 18 September 1997. "Hollywood and Esquire in Privacy Dispute," *The New York Times.*

271 Quoted in Ehrenstein, David. *Open Secret*, p.114. Quite who these "many people" were was not revealed.

272 Quoted in Junod, Tom. October 1997. "Kevin Spacey Has a Secret," *Esquire Magazine.* It is unclear why Spacey made a distinction between "gay" and "homosexual" here; his dislike of "labels," perhaps?

273 Quoted in Pogrebin, Robin. 18 September 1997. "Hollywood and Esquire in Privacy Dispute," *The New York Times.*

274 Quoted in Coles, Joanna. 20 September 1999. "Joanna Coles in New York," *The Times.*

275 Quoted in Coles, Joanna. 20 September 1999. "Joanna Coles in New York," *The Times.*

276 Clarke, Roger. 28 January 2000. "New films," *The Independent.*

277 Macaulay, Sean. 27 December 1999. "Beauty and the beastly," *The Times.*

278 Frostrup, Mariella. 30 January 2000. "What a beauty! Mariella at the movies," *The News of the World.* Veteran critic Pauline Kael was one of the film's few detractors: "It buries us under the same anti-suburbia attitudes that were tried out in *Carnal Knowledge* and *The Ice Storm.* Can't educated liberals see that the movie sucks up to them at every plot turn?" Quoted in Woo, Elaine. 4 September 2001. "Pauline Kael, Influential Film Critic, Dies at 82," *The Los Angeles Times.*

279 Howell, Liz. 4 February 2000. "In any one year, there are lots of different films that get released, even more in any decade: good films, bad films, dreadfully dire films. And then there are films like American Beauty (Cert. 18) in a class of their own," *Hull Daily Mail.*

280 Quoted in Benedict, David. 25 April 2004. "Kevin confidential," *The Independent on Sunday.* Russo's seminal study of homosexuality in the movies, *The Celluloid Closet*, was first published in 1981: the number of prominent actors who have outed themselves since this date is still barely into double figures.

281 "GLAAD" is an acronym for the Gay and Lesbian Alliance Against Defamation, a media monitoring association co-founded by Russo in 1985.

282 The Best Supporting Actor category has had one openly gay winner: John Gielgud, who triumphed at the 1982 ceremony for his performance in *Arthur*.

283 Quoted in Fleming, Michael. October 1999. "Playboy Interview: Kevin Spacey," *Playboy Magazine*.

284 Quoted in Ehrenstein, David. *Open Secret*, pp.360-361. Spacey had in fact claimed to be "not gay," rather than "straight," in *Playboy*: a subtle distinction, but an important one.

285 Musto, Michael. 28 December 1999. "La Dolce Musto," *The Village Voice*.

286 Quoted in Rush, George, and Molloy, Joanna, with Marcus Baram and Marc S. Malkin. 2 January 2000. "Madonna, Carlos Tay Apart for Y2K," *The New York Daily News*.

287 Quoted in Bracchi, Paul. 20 April 2004. "Why is Spacey so secretive?" *The Daily Mail*. The pictures were apparently taken the day before the Oscar ceremony.

288 Quoted in Rush, George, and Molloy, Joanna, with K.C. Baker. 2 April 2000. "'Beauty' & the Beach for Spacey," *The New York Daily News*.

289 Quoted in White, Lesley. 19 December 1999. "Spacey's Odyssey," *The Sunday Times Magazine*.

290 See "Kevin Spacey" entry at www.wikipedia.org.

291 In September 1999, shortly before his *Playboy* interview was published, Spacey was spotted "making out with a brunette model type" atop a table in a London café: this was apparently not Ms. Dreyer. See Ehrenstein, David. *Open Secret*, p.360. Kevin was also linked to Italian model/TV presenter Angela Melillo, who bizarrely claimed to be "his fiancée," at this time.

292 Beane, Douglas Carter. *The Little Dog Laughed*, pp.9-10.

293 Quoted in Bliss, Sara. May 2007. "The Drama King," *Gotham*.

294 See, for example, Oddy, Jane. Spring 2000. "The Spaceman Cometh," *Hilton Guest*; Berens, Jessica. 11 November 2004. "Lost in Spacey," *The Telegraph*.

295 See Ehrenstein, David. *Open Secret*, p.361.

296 See Malkin, Marc S. 8 September 2002. "Spacey out in Fire Island," *New York Magazine*.

297 Spacey, Kevin. 23 September 2002. "Spacey: No Man on an Island," *New York Magazine*. Boise has been home to brother Randy since late 1992, which perhaps accounts for Spacey's selection of this particular city for his fictional funhouse job. Married and divorced three times, Randy now lives with his long-time partner Trish: they have been together since 1995.

298 Quoted in Ouzounian, Richard. 11 February 2003. "Sex queries anger Spacey," *The Toronto Star*.

299 Quoted in Gallagher, Paul. 5 January 2006. "Official Government Report: Kevin Spacey is Gay," *The Daily Mirror*.

300 Quoted in Rush, George, and Molloy, Joanna. 22 April 2001. "GLAAD tidings," *The New York Daily News*.

301 White, Lesley. 19 December 1999. "Spacey's Odyssey," *The Sunday Times Magazine.*

302 Armitstead, Claire. 18 November 1999. "The Nice Man Cometh," *The Guardian.*

303 Spacey is unbilled in *Se7en's* opening credits (listing his name would have diluted the impact of Doe's blood-soaked emergence from the taxi considerably, as by the time the movie reached the halfway mark the audience would be waiting for "Kevin Spacey" to show up); this seems to have been his idea. "It turned out to be a fantastic move...I got to be in a movie that made a gazillion dollars around the world and I didn't do a single interview, and they couldn't use my picture. It was hysterical!" Spacey said in 2000. Quoted in Jolin, Dan. February 2000. "Kevin Spacey interview," *Total Film,* issue 37.

304 Gleiberman, Owen. 29 September 1995. "Seven," *Entertainment Weekly,* issue 294.

305 Dyer, Richard. *BFI Modern Classics: Seven,* p.39.

306 Larsen, Ernest. *BFI Modern Classics: The Usual Suspects,* p.63. This is also reflected in Byrne's performance. As Keaton–the only member of the lead quintet with a visible female partner–stands outside the police station after his release, his eyes lock onto Verbal's from across the street, and he barely notices girlfriend Edie's declaration of love for him.

307 Quoted in Weinraub, Bernard. 7 September 1997. "Between Image And Reality In Los Angeles," *The New York Times.*

308 The woman is listed in the credits as "Jack's dancing partner" but is described in the *BFI Modern Classics* guide to the film as "Karen, Jack's dancing partner" (Dargis, Manohla. *BFI Modern Classics: L.A. Confidential,* p.92). In the source novel, which takes place over several years rather than the "few weeks" of the movie, "Karen" is a high school girl who Jack rescues from a dope-dealing musician as a favour to his old boss, earning himself a promotion. They meet up again when she is 22, date, and eventually marry. Jack is already twice divorced, and his triple addictions–booze, pills and pornography– make for a somewhat stormy union.

309 Baker (now the star of TV drama series *The Mentalist*) is listed in the film's credits as "Simon Baker Denny," however I have used the shortened version of his name here.

310 Dargis, Manohla. *BFI Modern Classics: L.A. Confidential,* p.70.

311 Quoted in Fleming, Michael. November 2002. "The Most Daring Director in Hollywood," *Movieline.*

312 Quoted in unknown. 3 September 1997. "'Confidential' commentary," *Spliced.*

313 Quoted in Jolin, Dan. February 2000. "Kevin Spacey interview," *Total Film,* issue 37. Spacey's friend John Swanbeck, who made his directorial debut with the movie *The Big Kahuna,* likewise stated: "The reason I so wanted to do [the

film] is that it is a story told almost entirely with faces and eyes, and Kevin's eyes, seen close up on a 40ft screen, show you the whole human emotional landscape at once." Quoted in White, Lesley. 19 December 1999. "Spacey's Odyssey," *The Sunday Times Magazine.*

314  Maslin, Janet.19 September 1997. "Film Review: The Dark Underbelly of a Sunny Town," *The New York Times.*

315  Quoted in Griffin, Nancy. October 1999. "No more Mr. Bad Guy," *Los Angeles Magazine.*

316  Quoted in Stockwell, Anne. 28 October 1997. "Kevin Spacey Confidential," *The Advocate.*

317  Quoted in White, Lesley. 19 December 1999. "Spacey's Odyssey," *The Sunday Times Magazine.*

318  Geoffreys was a New York theatre actor who made a few mainstream film appearances in the 1980s before diversifying into adult movies (his most famous role was the creepy "Evil" Ed Thompson in 1985 teen horror flick *Fright Night)*, while Bullock was Spacey's co-star in *A Time To Kill* (1996). Others who have been "outed" as possible Spacey paramours over the years include actress Bebe Neuwirth, singer Sheryl Crow, and actor Anthony Rapp.

319  Quoted in Smith, David. 25 April 2004. "Spacey: face in the crowd," *The Observer.*

320  Quoted in Jackson, Erik. 8-15 April 1999. "Lost in Spacey," Time Out New York.

321  Quoted in Churcher, Sharon. 25 April 2004. "Kevin Spacey's father was a sexual monster," *The Mail on Sunday*; it seems likely that Spacey's discovery of Geoff's homosexual tendencies has contributed to his reluctance to publicly acknowledge his own alleged same-sex relationships.

322  Quoted in Turner, Brian. 23 January 2003. "Spacey speaks to hopefuls in HUB," *The Daily.*

323  Quoted in Smith, Adam. February 2000. "Top Cat," *Empire Magazine.*

324  Leith, William. 16 February 2002. "Look, Dad, top of the world," *The Guardian.*

325  Quoted in Stahl, Jerry. October 1996. "Hollywood's King of Cool," *Buzz Magazine.*

326  Quoted in Smith, David. 25 April 2004. "Spacey: face in the crowd," *The Observer.*

327  Stahl, Jerry. October 1996. "Hollywood's King of Cool," *Buzz Magazine.*

328  Blacker, Terence. 21 April 2004. "Spacey's curious incident of the dog in the night-time," *The Independent.*

329  Lyttle, John. 31 May 1994. "On Cinema," *The Independent.*

330  Quoted in Clarke, Donald. 5 April 2008. "We need to talk about Kevin," *The Irish Times.*

331 Ross, Jonathan. 12 April 2002. "I hope *Bend it Like Beckham* will be an enormous hit. I felt so happy afterwards I wanted to hug a Sikh," *The Daily Mirror.*

332 Thomson, David. *The New Biographical Dictionary of Film*, p.827.

333 Graham, Renee. 18 March 2003. "Kevin Spacey's films: now, usually suspect," *The Boston Globe.*

334 Although *K-Pax, The Shipping News* and even *Pay It Forward* were considered possible Oscar contenders prior to release, critical opinion of the films declined sharply once they reached cinemas. The reviewer who suggested in October 2001 that "When ballots go out to Oscar voters early next year, Kevin Spacey could be competing with himself for a best actor nod" (Romine, Damon. 23 October 2001. "Kevin Spacey: Oscar Bound?" *USA Today* online) proved wide of the mark. Kevin did manage to obtain another Academy Award in 2001, however. He paid $156,875 at a Los Angeles auction for the Oscar won by composer George Stoll for the 1945 movie *Anchors Aweigh*–and promptly donated it back to the Academy. He was also awarded the Golden Apple by the Hollywood Women's Press Association, which (in Kevin's words) is given "to the actor with the most colorful personality, and with the greatest news impact which has enhanced Hollywood's glamorous image throughout the world in 2001." Quoted in Welch, Mike. December 2001/January 2002. "Kevin Spacey: Reaching for Quoyle," *Venice.*

335 Hard as it is to imagine him masturbating in the shower or sarcastically drawling "It's not like, 'Oops, where'd my job go?'" Hanks was reportedly the first actor offered the role of Lester in *American Beauty.*

336 Quoted in Fleming, Michael. February 2003. "The thinking person's sex symbol," *Movieline.*

337 Quoted in Leve, Ariel. 22 April 2007. "Man with a mission: feature," *The Sunday Times.*

338 Quoted in Wohlberg, Julie. February 2003. "A Lunch with Kevin Spacey of 'The Life of David Gale,'" *Cinema Confidential UK.*

339 Buckalew, Betty. 28 February 2003. "What happened to Kevin Spacey?" *The Daily Trojan.*

340 Tookey, Christopher. 14 March 2003. "Why David Gale deserves to die," *The Daily Mail.*

341 Ellen, Barbara. 28 February 2002. "A sodden waste of Spacey," *The Times.*

342 Quinn, Anthony. 1 March 2002. "Film: I've got that sinking feeling," *The Independent.*

343 Bond, Matthew. 16 March 2003. "Dangerous minds think alike," *The Mail on Sunday.*

344 The many characters portrayed by Spacey that are explicitly compared to "the Devil" include Iago in Chatsworth High's production of *Othello* (mid-1970s),

Milo Tindle in the play *Sleuth* (1983), Mel Profitt in *Wiseguy* (1988), Harry Kingsley in *Iron Will* (1994), John Doe in *Se7en* (1995), Keyser Söze in *The Usual Suspects* (also 1995) and Albert T. Fitzgerald in *The United States of Leland* (2003). In 1998, Spacey voiced Hopper, the leader of a tyrannical grasshopper gang, in the Disney-Pixar movie *A Bug's Life*: even in cartoon form he was cast as a baddie. Kevin parodied his villainous screen persona in 2002 by taking a cameo role as the megalomaniac mastermind Dr. Evil in the film-within-a-film *Austinpussy* (directed by Stephen Spielberg and starring Tom Cruise as toothy hero Austin) in Mike Myers's comic box office smash *Austin Powers in Goldmember.*

345 See, for example, Leyva, Ric. 24 July 1996. "Star Watch: Kevin Spacey Won't Let Success Spoil the Fun," *The Standard Times*; Griffin, Nancy. October 1999. "No more Mr. Bad Guy," *Los Angeles Magazine*; White, Lesley. 19 December 1999. "Spacey's Odyssey," *The Sunday Times Magazine*. This is a trait he shares with childhood idol Bobby Darin, who made several genre switches in his short musical career, and is one of the elements Spacey admires most about him. "[I] identify with the conflict that Bobby had, that many artists face, between professional expectations and personal freedom. Bobby chose personal freedom which cost him something in terms of his career, but I think he chose right." Quoted in Pratt, Steve. 20 November 2004. "Not just a walk in the park," *The Northern Echo.*

346 Whitty, Stephen. 28 April 2000. "More questions than answers to Kevin Spacey: Is he playing too many roles that take the same attitude?" *Newhouse News Service.*

347 Quoted in Dougan, Andy. 21 February 2002. "Say hello to Mr. Nice Guy," *The Glasgow Evening Times.*

348 *David Gale* certainly had good pedigree. British director Alan Parker was knighted the year before the film's release, Oscar nominated for *Midnight Express* (1978) and *Mississippi Burning* (1988), and helmed the classic Nineties movies *The Commitments* (1991) and *Evita* (1996). *The Life of David Gale* remains Sir Alan's last completed film to date.

349 Spacey has admitted to one on-set vice: a Ping-Pong table. "It's one of the greatest games ever," he said in 2007. "I'm a Ping-Pong nut. I play constantly… Whenever I'm on location, that's the one thing I always want." Quoted in Hickey. 16 April 2007. "The Express: Hickey," *The Express.*

350 Quoted in John, Heather. 9 September 2001. "Natural Selection: When It Comes to Career–and Style–Kevin Spacey Is an Expert Evolutionary," *Los Angeles Times Magazine.*

351 Quoted in Leask, Annie. 22 December 2001. "Hollywood star Kevin Spacey pinched my bum every night for 6 months," *The Daily Mirror.*

352 Quoted in Reiter, Amy. 7 January 2002. "Kevin Spacey: 'The Oscar Wilde of Our Time'?" *Salon*.

353 Quoted in unknown. 14 March 2007. "New Moon, big chance for Billy," *The Irish Independent*.

354 Quoted in Rafferty, Terrence. October 2000. "Kevin Spacey Needs A Hug," *GQ*.

355 Quoted in Ginsberg, Merle. November 2001. "Inner Spacey," *W Magazine*.

356 Quoted in Lemmon, Chris. *A Twist of Lemmon*, p.ix.

357 Quoted in White, Lesley. 19 December 1999. "Spacey's Odyssey," *The Sunday Times Magazine*.

358 Quoted in Gore-Langton, Robert. 31 March 2002. "The day I got Spielberg to double," *The Northern Echo*.

359 Model, Betsy. January/February 2002. "American Paradox," *Cigar Aficionado*.

360 Blacker, Terence. 21 April 2004. "Spacey's curious incident of the dog in the night-time," *The Independent*.

361 See Modderno, Craig. July/August 2006. "London Calling," *Hollywood Life*.

362 *Ordinary Decent Criminal* was one of the first films of Colin Farrell (billed here as Farrel). Colin was cast as a minor gang member after Spacey saw him in the play *In a Little World of Our Own* at London's Donmar Warehouse and recommended the young man for the part, also securing him an American agent. As one columnist snarkily noted some years later: "Farrell is now a major movie star, while Spacey's star has slipped considerably. One wonders if he regrets his move, for the handsomer, more virile Irishman is now getting roles that would have gone to Kevin." Byington, George, quoted in Hadleigh, Boze. *Celebrity Diss & Tell*, p.166.

363 Quoted in unknown. 28 August 1998. "I have been a nobody all my life...now I'm hired by Mel Gibson and starring with Kevin Spacey," *The Sun*. Spacey, while apparently having been involved in the casting of Mullan, is not in fact credited as a producer on the film.

364 Quoted in Pearce, Garth. 9 February 2003. "There's something about Kevin," *The Sunday Times*.

365 Quoted in unknown. 20 April 2001. "The hard man who longs to show his softer side," *The Daily Record*.

366 Quoted in Bendoris, Matt. 11 January 2007. "I based DCI Walker on Bogart and my dad...both hard wee b******s–Interview," *The Sun*.

367 Quoted in Caven, Ruth. 13 January 2008. "Personally speaking: Brendan Gunn–How I told Brad Pitt to mind his language," *The Sunday Telegraph*. Colin Farrell was amused by Spacey's feeble attempts to master the accent: "It made Tom Cruise in *Far And Away* sound like a true advocate of Irish history." Quoted in Millar, John. 29 April 2002. "Never mind my language," *The Scotsman*.

368 Dixon, Leslie. 16 July 2006. "Leslie Dixon: Mrs. Doubtfire, Overboard, Outrageous Fortune," *The Sunday Telegraph.*

369 Quoted in Weaver, Clair. 26 November 2004. "It's Kevin the crooner," *The Evening Standard.*

370 Quoted in Otto, Jeff. 15 December 2004. "Interview: Kevin Spacey," *IGN Magazine.*

371 Quoted in Cronick, Scott. 10 December 2004. "Kevin Spacey comes to A.C. to pay Darin homage," *At the Shore.* Darin was a staunch supporter of the civil rights movement and often vocal in his opposition to discrimination against black and Jewish people. It can perhaps be assumed that Geoff Fowler, whose extensive record library passed to his younger son after his death, was unaware of this aspect of Darin's character.

372 Quoted in Leigh, Wendy. 9 October 2004. "Bobby dazzler," *The Observer.* After several disagreements with Spacey about *Beyond the Sea's* focus, Friedman himself was asked to resign from the project.

373 See "Beyond the Sea (film)" entry at www.wikipedia.org for further background information on the film's long history in development.

374 Maslin, Janet. 17 January 1997. "In A Bar Slinging Slang," *The New York Times.* During shooting, some footage from the film was stolen from Los Angeles International Airport: after a televised plea from Spacey, it was eventually returned.

375 Quoted in Mills, Nancy. 12 December 2004. "A Love Song for Bobby Darin," *The New York Daily News.*

376 Dee's tearful retreat into a storage cupboard on her wedding night, for example, is never explained in the narrative. In reality, she was possibly as young as sixteen (her birth year is unclear as Dee's mother had lied about her age to enrol her in school early) and long the victim of sexual molestation by her stepfather. Her extreme youth and abusive childhood–admittedly difficult subjects to mention in passing–are not referenced in the film.

377 While Spacey's Darin appears fairly fond of Nina and close to her husband Charlie, Evanier's biography reveals that the real Bobby was openly contemptuous of the "crude" pair and fearful they would prove a liability to his career. Darin was horrified by the revelation Nina was his birth mother and never forgave her for the "betrayal"–the scene where a resigned Bobby publicly acknowledges Nina as his mom and sings a song for her has no basis in fact. See Evanier, David, *Roman Candle*, pp.14-16 and 192-195. Nina and Charlie's children, including two daughters only a few years younger than Darin that grew up in the same household, are not featured in *Beyond the Sea*.

378 Anticipating such censure, Spacey has a journalist approach Bobby early in the movie and ask: "Isn't the real truth he's too old to play this part?" "That's just

crap! How can you be too old to play yourself?" Charlie (Bob Hoskins) retorts. Kevin just smiles wryly: a nice touch.

379 LaSalle, Mick. 29 December 2004. "'Beyond the Sea' there's a great big ocean of awful," *The San Francisco Chronicle.*

380 Ross, Paul, and Ronay, Shebah. 21 November 2004. "Bobby dismal...Or dazzler?" *The News of the World* (Ross, by contrast, considered *Beyond the Sea* "cool, swinging and sexy...one of the best films of the year").

381 Quoted in Berens, Jessica. 11 November 2004. "Lost in Spacey," *The Telegraph.*

382 Quoted in McDougal. Dennis. 21 November 2004. "Kevin Spacey's Battle for Bobby Darin," *The New York Times.*

383 Quoted in McDougal. Dennis. 21 November 2004. "Kevin Spacey's Battle for Bobby Darin," *The New York Times.*

384 Ironically Foxx, who also won an Oscar for his performance as priapic soul legend Ray Charles, used original material rather than performing his own songs.

385 A talented vocalist–he crooned Johnny Mercer's "That Old Black Magic" for the *Midnight in the Garden of Good and Evil* soundtrack–Spacey has sung in public several times in recent years, notably at a John Lennon tribute concert in New York City in October 2001, which he also hosted. Kevin performed "Mind Games," one of Lennon's favourite tracks, in front of an audience that included Lennon's widow Yoko Ono, with what one reviewer described as "unexpected passion." See Gumbel, Andrew. 5 October 2002. "Kevin Spacey: An enigma, even as he steps on to the political stage," *The Independent.* The following month Spacey performed the Beatles tracks "Hey Jude" and "Blackbird" at an Old Vic benefit in aid of the victims of the 9/11 terrorist attacks, and received two standing ovations. "I had no idea Kevin Spacey could sing–but he was great, really fabulous," commented an impressed David Furnish (Elton John's partner). Quoted in Leitch, Luke. 19 November 2001. "Watch This Spacey As Kevin Steals The Show," *The Evening Standard.*

386 *Edison* was written and directed by former *Wiseguy* scribe/co-producer David J. Burke and it seems likely that Spacey agreed to appear on the strength of their past association (he also starred in one episode each of Burke's TV drama shows *Unsub* (1989)–which won him his *Henry & June* role after director Philip Kaufman saw it–and *Tribeca* (1993)). The film does contain one nice exchange: when crusty journo Freeman remarks that "I'm beginning to think I need a woman in my life..." Spacey dryly responds: "Well shit, don't look at me!"

387 Quoted in Pierce, Andrew. 14 June 2005. "Kevin Spacey–PS," *The Times.*

388 See "Old Vic" entry at www.wikipedia.org and the Old Vic's official website, www.oldvictheatre.com, for further background information on the theatre's history. The transfer from the 325-seat Almeida to the thousand-plus capacity Old Vic (necessary due to Iceman's great popularity) was personally supervised

by Spacey: "I asked if the Old Vic was available. Everybody's first response was yeah, well it's over on the South Bank. Audiences can't find it, you don't want to go there. And I said, well, they find Wembley, they fill Wembley. Can we go look? There was nothing playing here at the time and I walked on to the stage, looked out at the house and I knew instantly that was where we should come. Quoted in Spencer, Charles. 26 April 2004. "The Old Vic building itself seemed to speak to me," *The Telegraph*.

389 Spacey, Kevin. 14 January 2001. "Jason Robards: An Example, a Mentor, an Actor Above All," *The New York Times*. Robards, who shared Kevin's birthday, likewise also played Jamie Tyrone in *Long Day's Journey* and *A Moon For The Misbegotten*.

390 See unknown. February 2005. "Passion Players–*Premiere* Celebrates The Most Compelling Performances of 2004," *Premiere*.

391 Peter, John. 19 April 1998. "Giving up the ghosts: Drama," *The Sunday Times*.

392 Macaulay, Alastair. 28 December 1998. "THE ARTS: Stars light up the London stage: Alastair Macaulay flips through his notebook to look back at the highlights of a year in which he met his own Waterloo," *The Financial Times*.

393 Quoted in Haun, Harry. April 1999. "A Pipe Dream Realized," *Playbill*.

394 Quoted in Jackson, Erik. 8-15 April 1999. "Lost in Spacey," *Time Out New York*.

395 Pierce, Andrew. 4 February 2003. "Kevin Spacey to run the Old Vic," *The Times*.

396 Spacey's director in *Long Day's Journey*, Jonathan Miller, also held the post between 1987 and 1990, helming 17 productions on the famous stage.

397 Quoted in Celeste, Eric. 15 March 2008. "The Unusual Suspect," *American Way Magazine*.

398 Quoted in Dougan, Andy. 21 February 2002. "Say hello to Mr. Nice Guy," *The Glasgow Evening Times*.

399 Quoted in Smith, Alistair. 22 May 2006. "Unusual suspects–Kevin Spacey and the Old Vic," *The Stage Magazine*.

400 Quoted in Ferguson, Alasdair. 26 July 2002. "New movie is good news for Spacey fans," *The Express*.

401 Quoted in Stern, Sarah. 10 January 2000. "The American Patient," *Focus*, nr 2.

402 Quoted in Butler, Kate. 26 June 2005. "Fiennes to star in Faith Healer at the Gate," *The Sunday Times*.

403 Quoted in Pogrebin, Robin. 28 November 2000. "Spacey Putting His Money Where His Heart Has Been," *The New York Times*.

404 Mandelson, another political pal of Spacey's, had become friendly with the actor after attending an Old Vic party with him in October 1998: a relationship that predictably delighted gossip columnists ("Mandy" is gay and lives with a much-younger partner). "Notting Hill chums of Mandelson...are delighted that he has found light relief in the company of the charming American bachelor,"

noted one wag in 1999. Gerard, Jasper. 1 January 1999. "Support role: Diary," *The Times*. As Sharon Churcher observed when interviewing Kevin's brother in 2004, Mandelson, at least when sporting a moustache, does bear some resemblance to Geoff Fowler. See Churcher, Sharon. 25 April 2004. "Kevin Spacey's father was a sexual monster," *The Mail on Sunday*.

405 See Ewing, Jack. *Spacey's Brother*, p.311.

406 Appropriately, Kathleen is the first woman to receive a kiss from Spacey's Jim Williams in the Christmas party scene about 20 minutes into the movie, followed by the real Williams's nieces and sister: most of the extras in this scene are relatives or friends of Jim's.

407 Before this could take place, Spacey first had to overcome his mother's Christian Science-influenced aversion to medical procedures, which had prevented her seeking treatment ten years earlier when she suffered a stroke that left her blind in her right eye. Randy claims that he was the one who convinced Kathleen to agree, by telling her "we shouldn't let loved ones down by not taking responsibility for our own mortality." Quoted in Ewing, Jack. *Spacey's Brother*, p.383.

408 Variety staff. Posted 9 April 2003. "Obituary: Kathleen Ann Fowler," *Variety*.

409 See Ewing, Jack. *Spacey's Brother*, p.418.

410 See Ewing, Jack. *Spacey's Brother*, pp.413-414. Kevin did not inform any of Kathleen's friends of her death, taking an entourage of production staff from Trigger Street along to her funeral instead.

411 Spacey, Kevin. September & October 2004. "One Life to Give," *AARP Magazine*.

412 Quoted in Welch, Mike. Fall/Winter 2001/02. "Hide and Seek with Kevin Spacey," *Maxim*.

413 This refers to Darin's actual grandmother, Polly, rather than his biological mother (and supposed sister) Nina. Evanier's own biography of Darin confirms that Polly was far from the vibrant, energetic woman portrayed by Blethyn in *Beyond the Sea*: "Polly, because of her morphine addiction and physical problems, was bedridden most of the time from her mid-40s on, subsisting on almost no food but zwieback and milk. She must have been a withdrawn, removed figure to Bobby, as much as she loved him and tried to be attentive." Evanier, David, *Roman Candle*, p.16.

414 Quoted in Mills, Nancy. 12 December 2004. "A Love Song for Bobby Darin," *The New York Daily News*.

415 Quoted in Mills, Nancy. 12 December 2004. "A Love Song for Bobby Darin," *The New York Daily News*.

416 Quoted in Wolf, Matt. 10 October 2004. "Arts: A Man For All Rhythms: Kevin Spacey explains why his Bobby Darin film is personal," *The Observer*.

417 Quoted in Welch, Mike. December 2001/January 2002. "Kevin Spacey: Reaching for Quoyle," *Venice*.

418 Quoted in Pryor, Cathy. 18 February 2007. "Watch this Spacey," *The Independent on Sunday*.

419 Brantley, Ben. 13 September 1998. "CRITIC'S CHOICE; High Hopes for Three Chameleons," *The New York Times*.

420 It later transpired that the phone Spacey was relieved of was not in fact his own: he had borrowed it from *Beyond the Sea's* producer Andy Paterson.

421 Quoted in Hampson, Katie. 19 April 2004. "Spacey 'comes clean' over mugging," *The Daily Mail* online. Kevin was taken to the accident and emergency department of nearby St. Thomas Hospital and released after receiving treatment.

422 Quoted in Wilks, Andy, and Carlin, Tom. 20 April 2004. "Spacey's shaggy dog story," *The Sun*. The actor took a different type of "cruise" in 2007 when he and some friends hired a narrowboat for a week to traverse the Kennet and Avon Canal, stopping off at several pubs along the way. "The thing I love about the countryside is you never quite know what you're going to get!" Spacey said. Quoted in unknown. 31 August 2008. "Dotes on a small island: Bigger Picture," *The Sunday Times*.

423 Quoted in Palmer, Paul. 22 April 2004. "Kevin's London beauties," *The Evening Standard*.

424 See, for example, Berens, Jessica. 11 November 2004. "Lost in Spacey," *The Telegraph*; Coveney, Michael. 11 September 2005. "I know I'm a big target," *The Observer*.

425 Spencer, Charles. 29 September 2004. "Spacey's down the gutter with this stinker: First Night," *The Telegraph*. For good measure, Spencer added that the play was "as slick, superficial and as unappealing as its title."

426 They were not all well behaved during the shows though. Spacey later complained that many *Cloaca* performances were spoiled by "inconsiderate" theatregoers who loudly unwrapped sweets or failed to switch off their mobiles: perhaps an unwise comment, given his own recent phone-related difficulties. Kevin himself has not always been beyond reproach: the lifelong smoker annoyed health and safety officers when he refused to stop lighting up in the listed–and heavily timbered–building. "Spacey has not taken any notice and remains defiant. It's pretty hard telling Hollywood stars what they can and can't do," one anonymous expert fumed in 2005 (quoted in Walden, Celia. 10 March 2005. "How Fellowes plans to follow up Oscar glory," *The Telegraph*). The officer presumably got his wish in the end, as the 2006 Health Act, which banned smoking inside enclosed public places, was introduced the following year.

427 *National Anthems* is an *American Beauty* for the Eighties: Spacey's blue-collar fireman gatecrashes the house of his social-climbing neighbours after a failed

party and gradually exposes their empty materialistic lifestyle. After appearing in the Long Wharf premiere–he was a last-minute replacement for future chum Al Pacino–Kevin bought the rights in the hope of staging the play again one day (a planned 1996 Broadway production fell through). Post-9/11, however, "greed is good" consumer-culture satire had begun to seem dated, which perhaps accounts for the mostly-poor notices the Old Vic's version received. "Times have changed," noted one reviewer, "and it seems bizarre to revive this parochial little play when the stakes are so much higher, and much more than capitalism is red in tooth and claw." Spencer, Charles. 9 February 2005. "Spacey's party piece falls flat: First Night," *The Telegraph*.

428 Spencer, Charles. 11 May 2005. "Spacey rides to the rescue at last," *The Telegraph*. Cary Grant portrayed the same character, languid playboy C. K. Dexter Haven, in the film version of *The Philadelphia Story* (which also featured Katharine Hepburn, for whom the leading female role of icy socialite Tracy Lord had been specially written) in 1940.

429 Spacey "played English" again in the 2009 film *Telstar*. As eccentric plastics importer Major Banks, the business partner of maverick Sixties record producer Joe Meek, Kevin–moustachioed and surrounded by more Brit character actors than he was in *Beyond the Sea*–delivers a true *Monty Python*-esque stiff-upper-lipped performance light years away from his wooden Kirgo. "I loved late night films on television when I was growing up," he told an interviewer. "They would always show old British wartime films." Quoted in Palmer, Alun. 23 June 2009. "Part of me feels British now but the knife crime here is shocking," *The Daily Mirror*.

430 Segal, Victoria. 1 October 2005. "Theatre: this happy breed of man," *The Sunday Times*.

431 Quoted in Billington, Michael. 13 April 2006. "I knew we'd be put under a microscope," *The Guardian*.

432 De Jongh, Nicholas. 11 April 2006. "Is it time for Kevin Spacey to hand over his crown?" *The Evening Standard*. De Jongh had been one of the actor's harshest critics from his first season. His *National Anthems* review starts with the words: "I BEGIN to have serious doubts about whether Kevin Spacey is the right man to run the Old Vic…" De Jongh, Nicholas. 9 February 2005. "Spacey's new Anthem is doomed to lie in doldrums," *The Evening Standard*.

433 Quoted in Billington, Michael. 13 April 2006. "I knew we'd be put under a microscope," *The Guardian*. Spacey's claims of unequal treatment found some support in the media. After the Press mauling of *National Anthems* another *Guardian* critic stated: "What worries me is that Spacey is being marked by higher standards than other performers. Something similar happened in the 90s to Kenneth Branagh, a big talent who was despised for some years in Britain: facing accusations of arrogance and ambition for commuting between

Hollywood movies and the London stage, and for seeking a career as an actor-manager in the tradition allowed in Britain only to Olivier." Lawson, Mark. 12 February 2005. "The Ken and Kevin show: Spacey is getting the treatment the press once dished out to Branagh," *The Guardian*.

434 Quoted in unknown. 13 April 2006. "Spacey fights on at Old Vic," *The Daily Mail*.

435 O'Neill, Eugene. *A Moon for the Misbegotten*, p.116.

436 O'Neill, Eugene. *A Moon for the Misbegotten*, p.131.

437 O'Neill, Eugene. *A Moon for the Misbegotten*, p.131. Jamie reveals that younger brother Edmund (who O'Neill modelled on himself), so sickly in the earlier play, is now married with a child: he appears to be the only Tyrone for whom the "journey into night" had a happy ending.

438 Quoted in Thorpe, Vanessa. 26 October 2008. "News: Spacey sets up a new golden age in theatre landmark," *The Observer*.

439 Hart, Christopher. 1 October 2006. "Starry, starry night," *The Sunday Times*.

440 Mamet, David. *Speed-the-Plow*, p.29.

441 Wolf, Matt. 19 February 2008. "Jeff Goldblum and Kevin Spacey are a near-perfect duo in Mamet's 'Speed-the-Plow,'" *The New York Times*.

442 Lloyd, John. 12 January 2008. "Television and radio: Sex and sensibility," *The Financial Times*.

443 Quoted in Martin, Nicole. 12 June 2008. "Kevin Spacey made professor at Oxford," *The Telegraph*.

444 Quoted in unknown. 24 November 2008. "My huge pride in turning round the Old Vic, by Kevin Spacey," *The Evening Standard*.

445 See Gans, Andrew. 9 March 2009. "Kevin Spacey to Receive Eugene O'Neill Theater Center's Monte Cristo Award," *Playbill*.

446 Quoted in Hiscock, John. 30 August 2008. "I'm taking the Old Vic global, vows Spacey," *The Telegraph*.

447 Quoted in unknown. 12 July 2006. "Super return," *The Westmorland Gazette*.

448 Quoted in Thorpe, Vanessa. 12 June 2005. "Kevin Spacey's Old Vic stage exit leaves fans feeling cheated," *The Observer*.

449 Quoted in Adams, Guy. 25 March 2005. "Pandora," *The Independent*.

450 Lister, David. 18 June 2005. "The Week in Arts: All change at the Old Vic 'not for the better,'" *The Independent*.

451 See Lister, David. 25 June 2005. "The Week in Arts: Kevin Spacey," *The Independent*.

452 Bradshaw, Peter. 14 July 2006. "Tights club: Brandon Routh makes a fine man of steel but it's Kevin Spacey who almost steals the show as Lex Luthor," *The Guardian*. A year later, Spacey appeared in the comic film *Fred Claus* as an "efficiency expert" determined to shut Santa's workshop down. When the

man in the red suit presents him with the Superman cape he always wanted as a child, all is forgiven and Christmas is saved.

453 Sandhu, Sukhdev. 14 July 2006. "A very superficial superhero: The new 'Superman' is great fun, with terrific special effects and a brilliant baddie–though its hero lacks personality," *The Telegraph.*

454 Spacey, Kevin. September 2004. "Center Stage," *Condé Nast Traveller.*

455 As one critic remarked in 2005: "When considering how good a film *The Usual Suspects* is, ask yourself this question–has there been a better thriller made in the 10 years since it came out? Not only is it the best of its genre–and indeed one of the finest films made in America in the last decade (and the competition is stiffer than you might think)–but when it is put in context of how it came about, it is nothing short of stunning." Unknown. 28 February 2005. "The Usual Suspects," *The Western Mail.* Among the "competitors" suggested by the writer of this article: *L.A. Confidential.*

456 As Stephen Armstrong noted in March 2008: "I've interviewed him before, and the first thing I notice is that he looks...well...relaxed." Armstrong, Stephen. 30 March 2008. "Why Kevin Spacey has never been happier," *The Sunday Times.*

457 As posted by Spacey, Kevin, on Twitter (www.twitter.com/kevinspacey), 17 June 2009.

458 Quoted in Mauro, Jeff. July/August 2006. "Kevin Spacey's balancing act," *Avery Cardoza's Player.*

459 As posted on the Old Vic's official website, www.oldvictheatre.com. The theatre also hosts an annual 24-Hour Plays event for industry professionals, usually fronted by Spacey. Past participants have included Brian Cox, Sanjeev Bhaskar, Rosamund Pike, Gael García Bernal, Susannah York, Jenny Agutter, Jim Broadbent, Saffron Burrows, Joseph Fiennes, Greta Scacchi, Josh Hartnett, Rufus Sewell, Nick Moran, Brooke Shields, Catherine Tate and Vince Vaughn: quite a diverse lot.

460 Quoted in Smith, Alistair. 22 May 2006. "Unusual suspects–Kevin Spacey and the Old Vic," *The Stage Magazine.* Spacey has a similar programme in place to encourage low-income families from the surrounding boroughs of Lambeth and Southwark to visit the theatre.

461 Quoted in Ewing, Jack. *Spacey's Brother*, p.420. Kathleen penned this poem in 1988, the year of Kevin's first noteworthy screen performances in *Wiseguy* and *Working Girl.*

Printed in the United States
by Baker & Taylor Publisher Services